Dedication

In memory of my maternal grandmother, Bubba, who taught me that life is five minutes and to my mother, Elaine, who knew how to live it.

Acknowledgments

The list of those who have gone before me shaping this new and exciting green business revolution is too long to print. Some, including Rachel Carson, my personal heroine, have been mentioned in these pages. But there have been many others, regular folk in various shades of green, who have, unknowingly, contributed through discussion and the kind sharing of ideas over the past decade and a half. To you, I say, thank you and please keep sharing. The more green that there is in the world, the more green that there will be.

I would like to single out a few people, without whom this work would not exist. Peter Archer, my editor at Adams Media, fought for a new kind of book on the topic of green business. I would like to thank my agent, Christi Cardenas, for her steadfast belief in the possibility of a green book born out of my experience. A special thanks goes to those that work in my companies for trusting in automation, embracing change, and for the willingness to try anything in the name of developing the ultimate green organization. My CEO, Mike, deserves particular recognition for living and working green every single day of his life. He keeps the wheels on the businesses and has been a steadfast green collaborator from the day that I met him.

To my family, I owe the deepest gratitude. Jeanne deserves a hug and extraordinary recognition for early reading and critique of this book. But more importantly she shares my belief that life's purpose is an opportunity to do good things in the world and has been the key to sustaining and inspiring me through my life's green journey. I would like to make a special acknowledgement to my dad, Roger, who always told me to go for it, living life to its fullest. A special thank you to my sister, Jen, and her husband, Dan, for teaching their daughter, Leah, that a green life is a life well lived.

EN
RK
RK

NE WHILE
OOTPRINT

Published by Adams Business, an imprint of
Adams Media, an F+W Media Company
57 Littlefield Street, Avon, MA 02322. U.S.A.
www.adamsmedia.com

ISBN 10: 1-59869-905-9
ISBN 13: 978-1-59869-905-0

Printed in Canada.

J I H G F E D C B A

Library of Congress Cataloging-in-Publication Data
is available from the publisher.

This publication is designed to provide accurate and authoritative information with regard to the subject matter covered. It is sold with the understanding that the publisher is not engaged in rendering legal, accounting, or other professional advice. If legal advice or other expert assistance is required, the services of a competent professional person should be sought.

—From a *Declaration of Principles* jointly adopted by a Committee of the American Bar Association and a Committee of Publishers and Associations

Many of the designations used by manufacturers and sellers to distinguish their product are claimed as trademarks. Where those designations appear in this book and Adams Media was aware of a trademark claim, the designations have been printed with initial capital letters.

The pages of this book are printed on 100% post-consumer recycled paper.

This book is available at quantity discounts for bulk purchases.
For information, please call 1-800-289-0963.

Contents

Part III. How Do I Get Them to Care?

Introduction

Going Green to Make Green

Life is five minutes, so get going!

I've always had a brain for business. I have also always had a passion for the environment and a longing to protect nature and the planet. But "green business" was an oxymoron when I was growing up in the early 1970s. It didn't exist. It was thought to be impossible to make money and care about the planet at the same time. Business owners created pollution and environmentalists yelled at them to clean it up. The government was somewhere in between trying to referee or broker a deal to make the most voters happy.

In the changing times of the 1970s, I had a life-shaping experience. In fifth grade I wrote a letter to President Nixon about the dangers of DDT (a particularly toxic and dangerous pesticide that was widely used) and felt empowered and responsible when the substance was banned a short time later. Eager and fresh out of business school in the early 1980s, I thought that my two interests of business and the environment were mutually exclusive. I was convinced that moving in the direction of a career in business meant that I had to choose sides and could no longer be an environmentalist. I couldn't have been more wrong.

In the early eighties, like so many of my generation, I focused on making money. I started a property management firm and worked like crazy to make my fortune. Although I started to make some serious money, I was burnt out, disillusioned, and felt there had to be more.

Then my favorite grandmother had a stroke. She didn't speak again until right before she died. As she lay there, taking her last few breaths, she seemed to be trying to say something to me. I leaned in, and she whispered, "Life is five minutes."

There are times when messages get delivered straight from the heavens, and for me, this was a lightning bolt. I knew I had to do more with my life, that it had a strong purpose, if only I could find out what it was.

Not long after this, a friend invited me to a meeting of Business for Social Responsibility (BSR). BSR is now a huge global organization with an incredible amount of influence over corporate and governmental policy as it affects ethics, people, and the environment. Back then it was just starting up. Unlike most entrepreneurial gatherings, there wasn't a lot of chest pounding and bragging. And, unlike a lot of environmental groups, there were no ideological histrionics—and no Birkenstocks either. Instead, it was a meeting of business leaders competing, not on their net profits, but on a different bottom line: social responsibility. What mattered to them was what they were doing for their community, employees, and the environment.

This was something I could get excited about. I strode back to my office and decided to start the first earth-friendly property management initiative. On that day I started greening my first business. It was a shift in my thinking. From that day forward, neither my business nor my life would ever be the same.

The Secret to Success

Today, I own several successful businesses and have been an entrepreneur for over twenty-five years. I'm here to say the secret to my success is green. I am a green business pioneer. In fact, I call myself an eco-preneur. I started greening my first business in 1992. This was before there was language to describe what we were doing. There were no how-to books, few earth-friendly suppliers, and no green consultants. Each time we sought a green solution to a problem, we started from scratch. Sometimes we succeeded, and at times we failed, but we never gave up. Slowly and painfully we discovered processes, products, and protocols that worked.

We developed one of the first systems in the United States for managing residential property in an earth-friendly manner. We also developed one of the first green office buildings in the country before the term "green building" was coined. In another streak of earth-friendly ingenuity, we came up with a software application that automated all of our communications and removed most of the paper and filing cabinets from our office. We didn't set out to invent things or be the first, but once we started thinking green, the creativity flowed and, eventually, so did the money.

I currently own five businesses, and each is built on earth-friendly foundations. They are stable, growing, moneymaking ventures that allow me to connect my head, heart, and spirit in a way that most people can only dream about. I'm living my passion, and my passion is making me a living.

Many people think that you have to sacrifice to get what you want. So if I'm balanced and happily running my business, I must be giving up something like money, right? Not true. You can be successful and responsible at the same time. Let's talk profit for a minute. My oldest venture, a property management firm with a green twist, makes a higher profit margin than most of my competitors around the country. A 5 percent profit margin is typical for my industry—we make around 20 percent. We've done this primarily by eliminating paper through automation—going green.

In addition to profit, loyal committed customers are another hallmark of a successful operation. We have retained many of the same accounts that we started with twenty years ago. This is an oddity in my industry in which there is often a customer revolving door. We have also grown our customer base 5 to 10 percent per year. That's real sustainability. Green breeds sustainable relationships and attracts customers who are often willing to find solutions rather than leave when there is a problem.

Green has also created a competitive advantage for us by drawing customers to us that are like-minded—other people who care. And there are more and more customers every day who are committed to green. My companies have often been perceived as more trustworthy and honest because of how we treat the earth. We have an ethic of treating the earth well, so our customers and suppliers believe that we will treat them well.

Committed and skilled employees are essential to any successful business. Two of my businesses are in the service sector, and human capital is what we sell. So having the best employees in the business is our competitive advantage. Being green has helped draw a staff that is empathetic, smart, kind, loyal, and committed to a cause of not only making money but doing so in a way that is also human healthy and planet friendly. Providing meaningful work is a perk that has great value to my employees and to my bottom line.

Green Is Not a Trade Secret

Judging from the number of confidential calls that I get every week, many businesses, big and small, are trying to figure out where to dive in to this new green ocean. In many of their voices I hear fear about not doing it right and attracting bad press or the dreaded ecosphere corporate-bashing bloggers. Many businesspeople simply don't know where to start. The green choices are perceived as too many, technical, and confusing. Some say there is a shortage of information and no obvious consultants to turn to. Others confess that their companies have such a long wish list of other things they want to do that green isn't a priority—yet. Still other callers complain that their leadership lacks green vision or a sustainable direction. They fear for the long-term health of the business as competitors go green and they don't.

I know firsthand that there is a thirst for green knowledge. Businesspeople crave to green their companies. So for the past several years, I have been sharing my knowledge, speaking with business groups, corporations, universities, and governments, helping them find ways to be green. Unfortunately, there isn't a formula. There is no one-size-fits-all approach because the players and operations

are so different. But what I've found in my own companies and
talking with dozens of other well-intentioned green wannabees is
that there is a commonality of process. Multinationals, one-per-
son shops, or medium-sized companies all share the same choices
when it comes to being earth friendly—scale and cash are the only
big differences. Whether you are a CEO, business owner, midlevel
manager, entry-level employee, or sole proprietor, all you need is
the knowledge of what is possible and the courage to act.

In these pages, you will find the secrets of what makes a business green and a step-by-step process for making it a reality in
your organization, no matter the size and no matter your role.
No smoke and mirrors or theoretical mumbo jumbo—just straight
talk from someone who has done it. This book is a "how to" guide
offering simple, clear language, with sections you can refer to when
you are ready.

The reality is that no company goes green all at once. Greening a business is a journey, not a destination. It's a marathon, not
a sprint.

The first section of the book will give you background on the
who, when, what, and where of green. I want to help you understand a seemingly new, fundamental shift in business. The second
section is a practical "how to green your business" guide, based on
an organization's key functions:

> The physical space

> The operation

> The product or service

You will find that the basics of greening the physical space are
fairly elementary, but the basics are a good reminder of all that
can be done. They are an accessible starting point for greening
neophytes, because they're the low-hanging fruit of greening any

organization. The concepts are well evolved, easy to understand, and can be quickly implemented. The sections on the operation and products are more imaginative and fun, containing unique green ideas that will challenge traditional business thought. Those who have already begun their green business transformation will be inspired to do more.

The third, and final, section will give you critical information to sell green up and down the ranks of your company, as well as to the outside world. It will also help you understand the pitfalls of greening an organization, so that you can avoid time-consuming or image-tarnishing mistakes. I'll share invaluable tidbits about what has and hasn't worked over the years in my organizations. The last chapter will summarize the concepts in the book and provide simple step-by-step instructions for how to get started greening your organization.

Green Your Business is a short cut for those who have the green will but not the time to find an answer through trial and error. What has taken me decades to learn, you can start doing immediately. Today, green is a market differentiator. Tomorrow, green will be the *only* way to survive in business.

Part I
Why Should I Care?

Chapter 1

Irresistible Reasons to Green Your Business

There are many rational reasons to green a business, but the reality is that most businesses and organizations don't start greening based on rationality at all. They do it because "everyone else seems to be doing it, so we should too." There's nothing wrong with this line of thinking. It is as good of a reason as any to begin the process. Some would have us believe that only moral or altruistic reasons are good reasons to green. Nothing could be further from the truth. There are many reasons to go green, and none of them are bad.

The environmental community has been trying to figure out for years how to get organizations and individuals to embrace basic green behaviors like resource conservation and recycling. They have tried shaming us, taxing us, dangling cost savings, and educating us with a religious fervor, but for a long time nothing seemed to work. The majority of the population resisted doing what seemed rational and right. It was only recently that behaviorists figured out—in the wake of people adopting green behavior en masse— what was going on: peer behavior is what drives green behavior. An industry-leading company that begins to go green will inspire other businesses to do the same. It is herd mentality—most of us don't want to be the first to adopt something new, but we don't want to be the last either. We want to be safe and in the middle of the pack.

If you happen to be one of the first to explore green in your industry or market space and are moved to action by solid rational explanation in addition to a little guilt and money dangling, then read on. There is truly every reason in the world to pursue sustainability and absolutely no downside—unless fame, success, and fortune is a downside for you.

Money Reasons

The price of gasoline is high and increasing rapidly. Natural gas prices are increasing faster and higher than ever, climbing by more than 50 percent from May 2007 to May 2008. Water prices have, in some cases, doubled over the past decade, particularly in dry areas of the Southeast and Southwest. We are also being charged more for what goes down the drain and the water that runs off our property. A few decades ago, electricity was advertised as "penny cheap" so that we would be enticed to use more. Now it is "dollar expensive." Even so, because we use so many electronic gadgets in our homes and offices, rates of use are still climbing.

There is no end in sight either to the demand for these resources or the speed at which their costs are escalating. It is simple economic theory—more and more people are chasing a shrinking limited supply of the earth's resources. To put our consumption into a global perspective, in the United States we make up only 5 percent of the world's population yet consume 25 percent of the world's resources and create 40 percent of the world's waste. In green jargon, we have a very large environmental footprint. Simple logic tells us that if we can reduce our resource use, it will cost us less. Additionally, if we can switch not only to resource-saving technologies but also to renewable resources, we can have an unlimited supply of what we need with more than enough to go around.

Currently, one of the ripest opportunities to save resources and money by going green is in energy-saving and renewable technologies. Because energy prices are escalating and energy-saving technologies have improved and become cheaper, payback periods (the number of years to recoup in savings the up-front money paid to upgrade) have been reduced to two to five years. As equipment costs come down while energy costs continue to rise, this payback period will only get smaller making it even more appealing to switch to energy-saving technologies. There are also financing packages available that fund energy improvements with payback terms based on the energy savings. Reducing energy use is a big green win; not only does it cut operating costs but it also proportionately reduces greenhouse gas emissions and air and water pollution from the power plants that supply the power.

Green improvements to an office or facility can also have a positive impact on other seemingly unrelated costs like insurance and liability claims. Insurance companies have begun looking for ways to give preferential treatment to buildings that are more sustainable. Premiums may be lowered because green buildings are built to last and tend to hold their value better with lower operating costs. Anyone in commercial real estate knows that reduced operating expenses will add to the net operating income and increase the building's value. As for potential liability claims, it is only a matter of time before insurance companies recognize that these claims and their associated expenses will decrease with cleaner and greener operations and products.

Revenue Benefits

Being green can increase revenue for your business. In this day and age of heightened green awareness, customers expect green products and service options and will even pay more for them. In many mainstream consumer markets, a company that does not offer an environmentally preferable version may find itself out of the running with many consumers. In other industries, green is still considered a niche or a novelty. So if your firm is the first to go green, this can be a market differentiator, setting your offering apart from others and drawing customers. Either way, green can strengthen your revenue by making your offering stand out or by keeping the customers who expect it.

Carbon Trading

Carbon trading is another potential way to bolster revenue in the future for the green organization. A company can reduce its carbon footprint by switching to renewable energy technology that cuts down on carbon energy consumption and emissions. If the reduced emissions are under specific limits—yet to be established in the United States—companies could conceivably sell their surplus pollution capacity, called *carbon credits*, to a company that hasn't been able to reduce its own carbon footprint. Until there is an official carbon trading market in the United States, it may be possible to sell carbon credits in Europe. Undoubtedly other resource-saving trading markets will develop over time to solve new challenges like water shortages. The organizations that have already started to plan for this new source of revenue by reducing resources will be in the best position to benefit from the developing trading markets when the time comes.

Green Staff

Another quantifiable bottom-line benefit of going green is the positive affect that greening has on staff in the organization. The U.S. Green Building Council (USGBC) has statistics that show people who work in a green facility have as much as 24 percent increased job satisfaction. The USGBC also says that productivity of workers can rise by as much as 10 percent. For some labor intensive companies a 1 percent improvement in worker productivity is financially comparable to eliminating its entire energy bill. If that weren't enough, when workers are happier and more productive that can also have a measurable effect on the bottom line by reducing absenteeism as much as 45 percent according to the USGBC.

Workplace Happiness Means Big Bucks

The issue of workplace happiness as it relates to the bottom line has become a hot topic because human capital is one of the largest expenses in organizations. The Gallup-Healthways Well-Being Index (*www.well-beingindex.com*) released in April 2008 found that workers who are unhappy take as much as an extra fifteen sick days a year. That adds up to a total cost to U.S. business of $14 billion in wages each year. Elements of a negative work environment that can contribute include job dissatisfaction, lack of trust at work, and authoritative rather than collaborative leadership. Greening your business operation, including your people, policies, and procedures, can go a long way to rid your organization of these negative contributing factors and result in happier, more engaged employees. A green organization is based on collaboration, authenticity, and meaningful work.

Going green equals a qualified and engaged work force. Hiring is a fifty-fifty proposition; half the time it works out and half the time it doesn't. People with green values are attracted to green companies, so employees are more likely to be a good fit when they know that your company's mission involves the environment. Having a waiting list of people who want to work for you is invaluable and can reduce the time and expense that it takes to find and hire qualified employees.

The financial upshot of greening an organization is quickly becoming a must have for every business. It has become the fiscally responsible thing to do because it can increase revenue and decrease expenses. And that is what business is in the business of doing—maximizing profits for its shareholders. Greening eliminates waste, risk, and can create a happier workplace, making it possible to make or save real money translating into more profit. And we all know those green profits will be more important as resource costs increase. Green truly does mean *green*—money.

People Reasons

Businesses are made up of people doing their jobs so they can live happy and healthy lives. Protecting the good health of people in our organizations is also a convincing reason to go green. Since World War II, when the chemical industry began to replace natural solutions with petrochemicals, we have been living in a chemical stew. The National Cancer Institute announced in 2004 that a woman's lifetime risk of breast cancer is now one in seven, double the one in fourteen lifetime risk in the 1960s.

Chemicals known as endocrine disrupters are found in many household products, pesticides, flame-retardants, and even personal care products. Though not at sufficiently high levels to cause cancer, these chemicals can interfere with the development of a fetus and cause issues with the health, intelligence, and future fertility of the baby. Possible problems caused by these chemicals include:

> Early puberty

> Imbalanced sex ratios

> Infertility

> Breast and testicular cancers

> Learning disabilities

> Behavior disorders

> Neurological conditions

Given the increase in incidents of these and other health issues, environmental health is fast becoming a growing area of study and concern. With time and technical advances, the chain of custody for cancer-causing chemicals will only grow. Imagine the resulting lawsuits against companies that put their employees or consumers knowingly or even innocently in harm's way.

This prospect has caused a growing number of scientists, business-people, and environmental health experts to look at toxins in a new way: from a green business prospective. In the past—and often still today—scientists, government officials, and businesspeople tended to ask, "How much harm is allowable" when assessing the risk of a specific chemical that might be toxic. They spoke in terms of "allow-able parts per million" when deciding if a toxic substance should be removed from a product. The reality is that consumers may not want *any* toxin in a product. When a business asks, "How little harm is possible?" the maker of the product rather than the consuming public bears the responsibility for ensuring the product is safe. A green business is proactive in preventing harm and protecting health.

Chemical pesticides, cleaning products, paints, and dyes are used in buildings and manufacturing processes around the world, with little regard for the resulting pollution and its effect on people inside or outside. Green alternatives and processes reduce or eliminate petrochemical products and effluents, resulting in a healthier work environment and cleaner air and water. Business has a newly anointed ethical responsibility to not put workers or consumers at risk for their health. Greening every aspect of an organization can significantly reduce those risks caused by human-made chemicals.

Employers and Employees

Many boardrooms around the globe are starting to discuss going green. No matter the size of the organization, executives are trying to figure out what they should do to make their organization greener. In most industries the peer pressure among executives has become a real turning point even if green efforts are still in the planning stages and on the down low. Employees who understand this and can help with greening their organization will have more opportunity for advancement as the executive team reaches out for help within its organizations.

Similarly, employees are beginning to expect green from their employers. A survey conducted in late 2007 by Adecco, a New York-based provider of work force solutions, found that more than half of the respondents thought their company should be doing more for the environment. Thirty-three percent of the employee respondents said that they would be more inclined to work for a company that is environmentally conscious.

There is also a whole new group of Generation Yers entering the work force who list the environment among the top three things that they are concerned about. In fact, people of all different age groups want more than pay from their work—they want meaningful work. Meaningful work is a reason to get up in the morning that transcends a paycheck. It means doing good things that help rather than harm the world. Greening your organization can provide meaningful work for those that are looking for it.

Good Neighbors

Being a good neighbor is another reason to throw caution to the wind and begin greening efforts. Every business is part of a community whether it chooses to recognize this fact or not. Each business decision, from hiring to what is done with your business's waste, affects the community in which you operate. Green facilities have lower impacts on the communities because sustainability initiatives take into account fair treatment of all stakeholders. A company's greening efforts, no matter where it is located in the world, will elicit a more favorable image when it is a positive force in its community instead of a passive and uncaring one. Parts of the world previously considered remote are no longer so because almost all workers have access to cell phones, and more and more are linked into the Internet. Companies can no longer hide poor treatment of workers. Word can easily get out if an operation is less than community or employee friendly.

While new laws and codes favor businesses that use green techniques in building, you can bet that tax incentives or special programs for businesses that use fewer resources and pollute less will soon follow. Governments around the world are moving in this direction, due to hot-button issues like global warming. The organizations poised to take action on these incentives now will be ready to reap the benefits when the time comes.

Planetary Reasons

Protecting the ecosystem seems like a selfless reason to green an organization. It's self-serving too and rooted in something much more important than profit or even people—our survival. Protecting and preserving the ecosystem is connected to supporting our way of life, including commerce. To understand this, it is important to realize that we are encountering some of the most daunting challenges that humanity has ever faced. It will make pestilence, plague, and famine from biblical times seem like a cakewalk. Dwelling on environmental problems in order to frighten people is not productive, because people may feel too paralyzed to act. The problems may seem far too large for any one business or one person to cure. But we need to start somewhere, and to start we need to identify the issues to solve the issues. So the first issue we need to talk about is the increasing population.

In the 1920s the human population of the planet was about 2 billion. It took *Homo sapiens* 100,000–200,000 years to climb to that number. By 1960, just forty years later, the number of people had swelled to 3 billion—a billion more people on the planet. Around the year 2000, another forty years later, the population had doubled again to 6 billion human beings. By 2010 the population will be headed to 7 billion, with 9 to 10 billion expected by 2050. According to the World Bank and the United Nations in 2008, approximately one-fifth of the people on the planet are living in abject poverty, malnourished, and without clean drinking water. If there are not enough resources to feed, clothe, and shelter one and half billion people today, what will happen when there are 9 or 10 billion people on the planet? Simply stated, a frighteningly large number of human beings are chasing a limited quantity of resources. Tomorrow more people will chase that same limited quantity of resources.

This is a big problem, and you might be thinking, "What am I supposed to do about this global problem? I can't do anything about this!" Ah, but you can. If your business can figure out how to use resources more effectively, there will be more to go around. If businesses reuse rather than discard, we can employ the same resources over and over. Limited resources is a problem business can help solve.

Climate Change

Another scary issue is the climate. Everything that we do—driving, heating or cooling our homes, making products, and nearly every modern convenience we have—is created and maintained by burning carbon. Gasoline-powered engines, coal-burning electrical plants, and natural gas furnaces fuel our growing needs and spew greenhouse gases into the atmosphere accelerating planetary warming. The worst-case scenarios predict coastal flooding, epic droughts, famine, monster storms, and destruction around the globe.

Some experts say that we have a twenty-year window to fix the problem, and others say longer, but most concur—we've got trouble. Right here on our planet. If we don't start dealing with it soon, we're endangering the survival of many species on Earth—including our own. Businesses are directly part of the problem and can be part of the solution by beginning to green their buildings and operations, thereby reducing their carbon footprint.

Fresh Water

Many believe that we will figure out how to stop global warming, but fast on the heels of that solution will be a much more daunting challenge—enough fresh water. Climate change and population increases are impacting water supplies worldwide. Ground water accounts for about 25 percent of the earth's fresh water. Surface waters store only about 1 percent, leaving the balance of the earth's fresh water in polar ice and glaciers. Population pressures are diverting and shrinking surface water, and pollution is threatening ground water resources, leaving us with huge potential shortages in the not-too-distant future.

Everything we do is connected to water. We use enormous amounts in our homes and workplaces. We also use it to make electricity, plastic, cotton, and everything else. Power plants alone consume 40 percent of the United States' fresh water. Redesigning products and processes to use less water in their manufacturing and during consumer use of the end product will become an increasingly critical function for green business. As well, we'll need to invent new technologies to clean polluted water and recycle it.

Okay. We're done with the scary part. I listed these planetary reasons to go green to highlight some of the more critical threats. It is disconcerting that all of these potential threats are coming together on our watch, but there is good news. We, as a species, are very clever. We are smart, innovative, and creative. We possess the ability to figure our way out of this mess. As my father once said to me when I asked him for money for my business long ago, "You got yourself into this, and only you can get yourself out of it."

We can get ourselves out of this problem if we all work together to green our own organizations and help others to green theirs. Business, nonprofits, government, and citizens need to look at their own sphere of influence and start to do what can be done.

Personal Reasons

Some of the best reasons to green an organization are for strictly personal feel-good reasons. One of the best ways to relieve eco-anxiety—the fear that all is lost because we are in such an environmental mess—is to do something positive for the environment. Certainly, taking on the responsibility to help green the place that you work will go a long way to cure any eco-anxiety that you might be feeling. And by involving your coworkers you can help cure their eco-anxiety pain as well.

Do It for the Kids

Do it for the children. Many people change a behavior like smoking because their kids want them to. This can be a good reason to green your workplace—your kids. Most kids intuitively understand that we need to take care of the planet and everything on it. Many learn about protecting the environment in school, and others just somehow *know* that we need to take care of the earth.

Our kids will be living in whatever we leave. Greening can be philosophical. The Great Law of the Iroquois Confederacy, the oldest living democracy on earth, adhered to this philosophy of "do it for the kids." The Great Law advised us to take care of the next seven generations and not just the current one. Let's be honest. Our society frequently focuses on our families in the here and now. If we consider our family and descendants many generations into the future, we may make different decisions about the environment and our daily choices. The more that we can solve our environmental problems, the better shape we will leave the planet in for our children and their children.

It's really all about legacy. So do it for your legacy. When you are involved in greening an organization, you have something to show for it. You can point to that company and say, "I helped make those changes." If you own the company, you have all the more reason to make greening a part of your legacy. The early green adopters will be considered pioneers and will be long remembered in their industry.

Love and Happiness

Do it for love and happiness. Yes, that's right: love and happiness. Greening taps into our human need to get and give love. It is, by definition, a nurturing act of kindness to yourself, others, and the planet. For the same kind of reasons that people do volunteer work, greening can make us happy. This hit home for me one day when I was interviewing a college student who was involved in a student green housing project. The project was loads of additional work for him on top of an already overbooked college semester, and I asked him why he was involved in the program. He told me that it made him happy. It made him feel good to do green things—it was that simple. Having a hand in greening an organization has the power to make you feel good.

Do it to release your creativity. Green is also about an opportunity to be creative. It is the chance to make the workplace exciting and new by reinventing and rethinking how everything is done. It gives us the power to ask why we are doing things and the ability to make things better. It can give the same old business new life and new meaning for everyone involved in the organization.

The Right Thing

Do it because it's the right thing to do. We know that business is part of the problem, and we know it needs to be part of the solution. In fact, some businesspeople would find it immoral to ignore the consequences of their actions with respect to the environment. To avoid greening is to be subject to shame and disgrace in the eyes of many. Yes, this gets a little heavy, but there are people who are motivated to green based on a moral rather than business decision.

As you can see, there are many reasons to begin the greening process in your business. You don't need to feel all warm and gooey inside about all these reasons—one will do. Some people get hung up on the motivation for businesses turning green—as if it is somehow less worthy to be greening for profit rather than altruistic reasons.

There is nothing wrong with enlightened self-interest. It is what has brought us the many modern conveniences that we enjoy today. The attitude that there is gold in green may just get us through the overwhelming environmental challenges we are facing. You need to find the reasons that motivate you to go green; ultimately you must find reasons that will resonate with those working around you. There is a shift going on in the world of business. A new golden age of green business is coming, and no one should miss it.

Now that you have good reasons to green your business, the next two chapters will give you critical background information for your greening journey. You will find out what green means in our culture and who is green in the United States. You will even begin to understand that people, businesses, and products come in different shades of green.

Chapter 2

The Green Revolution

Post–World War II prosperity was humming along in 1962 when a shy scientist and nature writer, Rachel Carson, published her book, *Silent Spring*. The book told a parable about a future spring with no songbirds because of the relentless and careless use of chemical pesticides, particularly DDT. Carson's sound scientific research and convincing prose gained the affection of the media and the public. She was eventually asked to testify before Congress on the subject of chemical pesticides. Many considered her a heroine for going head to head with the chemical industry, ultimately winning by bringing visibility to the dangers.

In addition to killing birds, DDT is considered a possible human carcinogen, and many doctors suspect it causes pancreatic cancer. It has also been found to mimic and disrupt reproductive hormones in both lab animals and male alligators. The government banned DDT in 1972, but it is still used in other countries to kill mosquitoes for malaria control. To this day, DDT shows up at unsafe levels in human breast milk in those countries where it is still being used. Little did Carson know that she would be the catalyst that launched the modern-day environmental movement, leading to a potentially much larger revolution, the shift to green commerce.

The discussion that Rachel Carson started about DDT stirred emotions on both sides. Some farmers and one biologist ate spoonfuls of the stuff in front of cameras to prove that it wasn't dangerous to the public. By the late 1960s, thousands of college students and some politicians rallied for the earth, resulting in the first official Earth Day in 1970. The Back to the Land Movement (made up of radicalized youth) joined forces with the Vietnam War protestors. Both groups initially were on the fringe but gave visibility to the issues that eventually brought environmentalism into the mainstream. The government caught the wave of early environmentalism by the early 1970s and created the Environmental Protection Agency (EPA). In that same decade, the federal government passed the Clean Air and Clean Water Acts. Each state formed agencies to police air and water pollution. Businesses with smokestacks and effluent pipes became regulated and hired a new breed of professional, environmental engineers, to ensure compliance with new laws and codes. These were the embryonic days of green business. This was the first time, on a large scale, that business became aware of a greater responsibility for environmental protection.

By the 1980s, a new type of organization began to proliferate to act as watchdog over the governmental agencies that regulated business—the environmental nonprofit or nongovernment organization (NGO). Groups like the Sierra Club, the Nature Conservancy, Environmental Defense Fund, and environmental law nonprofits grew their war chests and gained traction with the public. These groups originally formed to protect the environment from business and were often leery of both business and government motives. They were trying to protect the environment against the widely held corporate belief of the time: In pursuit of profit, business could do no wrong. The slash-and-burn, anything-goes 1980s and the preceding decades of pollution and resource use were so hard on the planet that the United Nations formed a group—the Brundtland Commission, formally the World Commission on Environment and Development.

The Brundtland Commission was chaired by Gro Harlem Brundtland, the first woman prime minister of Norway. It dealt with what many saw as the rapidly accelerating deterioration of our environment and the eventual dire consequences for society and the economy. The document the commission produced, *Our Common Future*, was the first international acknowledgement of global environmental damage. There was a new realization that pollution and resource use does not obey state or national boundaries and that all nations needed to work together on policies and solutions. The Brundtland Commission coined the term *sustainable development*: development that "meets the needs of the present without compromising the ability of future generations to meet their own needs."

"Sustainable development," or "sustainability," started to be spoken of by some businesspeople in the early 1990s. The concept particularly appealed to middle-aged, progressive entrepreneurs who found themselves running successful businesses but still longed to have a positive social impact. Between the Brundtland Commissions report and the early 1990s several new NGOs formed around the concept, attracting members from the progressive business community: Business for Social Responsibility, the World Business Academy, CERES, and the Caux Round Table. This was the beginning of a new way of thinking in business. It was possible, this new breed of businessperson believed, to do well by doing good—rather than being so focused on profit for profits sake. For the first time in U.S. business there was an authentic link between commerce and the overall well-being of not only society but also the planet. Some businesses started to think beyond mere compliance with environmental regulations to how they could become a force for good.

By the turn of the millennium this philosophy had spread, thanks to the Internet. More businesses and some consumer groups began to notice that some companies were doing things in a socially responsible way. A grassroots green movement picked up momentum, and many websites—for instance, The Green Guide (*www.thegreenguide.com*), and Treehugger (*www.treehugger.com*)— were developed to prod consumers to behave responsibly and buy green. Organizers hoped these efforts would push business to provide more green products and services. Some NGOs even began partnering with corporations that were launching green initiatives and products. By late 2007 the media began to pick up on this new green momentum, and green coverage went mainstream. Suddenly, the world seemed greener than before. Green talk inspired more green talk and gave birth to a new era of green commerce, as action began to follow from both consumers and business.

Green Defined

The term green, meaning environmentally friendly, has only come into our lexicon in the past few years. It is less technical than sustainability, which is a mouthful and poorly understood by the average person. In one focus group that I was watching in the spring of 2008 in New Jersey, a participant thought that the term sustainability meant, "won't stain," and another assumed it was a product that was built to last, having nothing to do with the environment. Likewise, the phrase environmentally friendly, which was used for decades, now sounds antiseptic and impersonal. On the other hand, green to most people clearly means the environment, which is why the media and many others have chosen it as the preferable term. Green is accessible and not loaded with other polarizing meanings. Even though there is the Green Party, green is not typically associated with political persuasion.

Even so, green can be confusing because it is used as a catchall for a complicated set of concepts. To simplify, think of green as anything that conserves our natural resources while protecting the ecosystem. For example:

> All things grown organically, without petroleum-based chemicals, are green. These can range from our food to organic cotton.

> All things natural, meaning not made from petroleum but from raw materials grown or found in nature, are green. So clothing made from soybeans is natural and green.

> Any renewable resource, like sunshine, wind, and water, is also considered green when used to power homes and factories.

> Products, coatings, and processes that are less toxic or nontoxic are also considered green; for instance, non-petroleum-based cleaning products, low V.O.C. paints, and bio-based plastics.

> Recycled content is green, and so is the term recyclable.

> A technology, product, or service that saves energy, water, or any resource is green. Fair trade products are deemed green.

These are but a few examples of the diverse uses of the term *green*.

There are no human-made perfectly green products, services, or processes yet. Everything that we produce requires energy, typically from a nonrenewable source. This ranges from energy used in the manufacturing process to the energy expended in the maintenance or use of the object. Many environmentalists think that an environmentally friendly car is an oxymoron; even if a car is partially powered by renewable energy, it still took an enormous amount of nonrenewable energy to produce the car in the first place. But generally speaking, green implies that the product or service is made, operated, or provided in a way that does as little harm to nature as currently possible.

Green Labeling

How green something is depends on how many elements of green it contains or how little it harms nature. A locally farmed, organic strawberry grown on a farm using only wind power as the energy source and transported by bicycle to market is greener than an organic strawberry shipped from South America by airplane—even though both are grown organically. In time, products will be graded by greenness on a defined scale. When that happens, consumers will be able to make informed choices using a label, similar to the one we use now for nutrition elements, that will provide specific environmental indicators for each product. In concept, each product will list the environmental harm caused by the production, transportation, and use of the product. The label will include indicators like greenhouse gases emissions, water and raw materials used, and the amount of toxicity so that a consumer can comparison shop in shades of green. This type of green product rating system is a dream of many around the world will eventually become reality.

Green business would have been an oxymoron for much of the last century. Businesses belched pollution and poured garbage and sludge into oceans, rivers, and lakes without thought or remorse. It was just how things were done. Businesspeople thought the planet was big enough to absorb any pollution or waste we dumped in it. Today, green business includes the pursuit of zero pollution, minimization of resource waste, reduction of toxins, and less carbon intensity—not exactly sexy stuff. But what *is* sexy is the exciting and creative journey of how we get from here to there and who will be capable of making that journey.

What makes green business so compelling and earth-shatteringly refreshing is that it is far more than complying with environmental laws of the land or retrofitting a building to be more energy efficient. It is the process of figuring out how to do more with less in an organization. Yet it is more than just simple efficiency. Yes, it involves an engineering puzzle to redesign products, facilities, and processes, but there also is a large people component. Turning the people green—the employees, the suppliers, the investors, and the customers—is the real fun and where half of the benefits are realized when greening an organization. You haven't heard the last of this subject; I'll include much more on the definition of the green businesses in the next chapter, but first let's understand this overall green movement a bit more.

What Drives Us to Green

Green is not a fad or trend that will fade with time. It is a fundamental shift in the way we do business. The greening of America is being caused by a whole series of events—one of which was attributable to Al Gore's movie, *An Inconvenient Truth*. This movie helped the public understand global warming in a way that nothing else had ever been able to do. His Oscar, Nobel Peace Prize, and the media attention the film garnered catapulted the issue into the American consciousness.

This new climate change awareness, combined with devastation from Hurricane Katrina, severe drought in much of the southern United States, and sky-high energy prices, created the conditions for green. Suddenly green had a foothold in the American psyche. Average, hard-working Americans as well as large and small businesses were being pinched between high gas prices and high utility costs. Environmental problems were suddenly hitting home. Business and consumers were both ripe for a green awareness pitch.

By the fall of 2007, the American mainstream media was bitten by the green bug and became an unexpected driver of environmental awareness. Every newspaper, magazine, and news show was suddenly carrying a weekly, if not daily, dose of green. Professional journals and trade websites began to pick up green stories and discuss what green changes should be made in their own industry. National Geographic bought The Green Guide, a website devoted to greening homes and consumers. NBC turned the peacock green periodically and added green content to many of its sister channels highlighting the network's newfound commitment to environmental responsibility. Sundance and the Discovery television channels both scheduled regular green programming, and in June 2008 the Discovery Channel launched Planet Green, a twenty-four-hour cable channel devoted to eco-friendly living. And in a highly publicized move, the 2007 Emmy Awards tried to move toward being carbon neutral, using solar power, hybrid cars for stars, and bikes for show staff.

With all of these converging factors and a heightened awareness, American business began seriously contemplating how to ride the green wave. Better late than never; most of the rest of the developed world had already started to green a couple of decades previous. The global economy meant that American products made for Europe and Canada faced stringent environmental requirements.

American companies changed product formulas and practices so they could sell in those parts of the world. Gradually, some of that greener product thinking transferred to the U.S. market where consumers were beginning to appreciate cleaner and greener products. The fact the multinational corporations were selling products both in the United States and abroad helped to drive green supply in the states. Now that the awareness was reaching a fever pitch in other parts of the world and with the American media going green, business was poised for a green explosion.

There has been much talk about whether this new green business phenomenon is a long-term movement or a trend that will disappear if energy costs retreat. Never fear—green business is here to stay. Once companies invest and convert their facilities and operations to be more resource saving and pollution preventing, they won't return to doing business in an unsustainable way. Even if energy prices drop, waste is waste, and savings are still savings. Once equipment, buildings, and practices are converted, it is fiscally unsound to undo changes and improvements. There is also considerable momentum to redesign products and services using green principles. Already businesses are competing to green more products and services, as consumer awareness pushes innovation and companies respond. Green will beget more green as healthy competition and a broader awareness become reality.

Investment money is also a green driver and a big reason that this trend will not stop. According to a study by Cambridge Energy Research Associates (CERA), worldwide investment in clean energy technologies alone could reach a total of $7 trillion through 2030. Some say that this new investment trend in clean or green technologies will easily dwarf the unprecedented dot-com investment era of the late 1990s. In addition to renewable energy technologies, green tech includes clean transportation, clean water, and green product development. Much of the investment world is betting that green will be a needed and highly successful vehicle for making money for a very long time.

The Market for Green

The market for green goods and services, while difficult to quantify in exact terms, is large (about one-quarter to one-third of all adult Americans) and growing. No one knows the exact numbers, because the market is based on a psychographic rather than a demographic. That is, it is behavior based rather than socioeconomically based on measurable demographics like age, sex, education, income, and politics.

The green market is also elusive in that it encompasses so many different behaviors: product buying habits, driving habits, child care, and the way we live in our homes. This makes it difficult to create a metric that could encompass all the different ways a person could be green. To complicate things further, green involves many different micro movements, such as the slow food movement, which is about enriching your life by buying food directly from a local community farm and savoring the experience of buying, making and sharing it with family and friends; and the simplicity movement, which is voluntarily simplifying life by not being attached to or having so many possessions which also has the effect of reducing resource use. Those who define themselves or others as part of the metro-spiritual movement see their purchases of environmentally friendly goods and their practice of yoga and meditation as a way to a better world. Likewise, the natural baby and natural childbirth movements are made up of parents who want to birth and raise their children without contaminants found in products and food. New movements tangentially related to and pushing the green movement are springing up all the time. Studies and statistics have been woefully inadequate when trying to get a handle on this burgeoning market.

However, there is some credible empirical data about the green market, garnered through studies done over the past decade. In 2000 Paul Ray, a sociologist, and Sherry Ruth Anderson, a psychologist, wrote a book, *The Cultural Creatives*, that was based on years of survey research studies of more than 100,000 Americans and more than 100 focus groups. They concluded that there are over 50 million Americans who care about ecology and saving the planet, as well as about peace, social justice, and spirituality. These "cultural creative types," as Ray and Anderson named them, cut across socioeconomic categories and religious and political affiliation, as well as age and sex. They are Republicans and Democrats, rich and poor, young and old, and of every religious background. What holds this group loosely together is that they care about positive social transformation.

Since Ray and Anderson's groundbreaking book, many have tried to update and further define this market. Lifestyles of Health and Sustainability (LOHAS), an organization that attempts to keep track of this market, has also conducted studies in conjunction with the Natural Marketing Institute. The studies found that the LOHAS consumers are a $207 billion marketplace that is likely to double in size by 2010. LOHAS consumers, sometimes referred to as Lohasians, are interested in buying products from companies that practice responsible capitalism. Product sectors that appeal to them include green building supplies, socially responsible investing, organic clothing and food, energy-saving devices, ecotourism, and green products and services.

Other groups, including many polling organizations, have also tried to define this market in numbers. Gallup Poll released the results of a green behavior poll for Earth Day 2008 showing that 28 percent of Americans have made major changes and 55 percent minor changes to their own shopping and living habits out of environmental concern over the past five years. Only 17 percent said that they had made no changes.

Similarly, the American Association of Retired Persons (AARP) also commissioned a green consumer survey of 30,000 of their members in late 2007 and found that there are 40 million "green boomers" in the United States—that is half of all baby boomers. Focalyst, the New York research firm, identified boomers by their environmental practices, such as buying organic foods, choosing locally produced goods, and supporting companies that are socially responsible. The study not only cast light on the number of green consumers in that demographic but also found, contrary to popular belief at the time, that a high income didn't predispose someone to buy green. Those boomers earning less than $50,000 a year were more likely to buy green than those earning more than $150,000 a year. Prior to this study, it was assumed that green consumers were more highly educated and had more disposable income than traditional consumers and were more willing and able to buy green.

The AARP study and others have identified green behavior on a color chart of brown (no concern for the environment) to deep green (deep concern for the environment and the behavior to match). The reality is that no person is perfectly green—people behave in shades of green. The definitions and color choices are subjective for each type of consumer on the spectrum. Some analysts believe the deep green and light green consumers are the LOHAS market and make up one-quarter to one-third of the adult population in the United States. Here's a brief summary of various shades of green consumers with their corresponding behavior:

Deep green—These consumers are the greenest on the planet. They understand the need for green, and their purchases match their values.

Light green—They have started down the green path and are on their way to living a green life. Some of their purchases and behaviors are already earth friendly. Their hue of green will deepen as they get more knowledge about all things earth friendly.

Khaki green—They think green some of the time and are just beginning to connect their shopping habits and daily living habits to being earth friendly. Saving energy and money drives their greenest purchases and behaviors.

Light brown—They are not yet conscious about living or buying green but are starting to be influenced, even if subconsciously, by the culture at large about making earth-friendly choices.

Brown—They are skeptical of the environmental movement and its values. Based on their principles and personality, they will not make any earth-friendly choices even if they save money or the choices are good for their families.

There are no statistics that directly give the number of consumers in each of the hues from brown to green. But there is evidence that light greens are moving toward becoming darker green, light browns are moving toward becoming khaki, and so on. The brown end of the spectrum is shifting greener as people are inundated with information about green and green technologies become more accessible and affordable. Life triggers also have an effect on the movement along this behavior spectrum. Someone who has a baby and may have been light brown in the past suddenly will jump a couple of shades greener to light green as he or she tries to protect the new baby from toxins in food and plastic bottles.

Realizing that people must learn or relearn green behaviors gives us an important insight into how to go about greening our organization, products, and services. Most people are moving along the spectrum to lead greener lives at home and at work. Some will resist it today, but they may not tomorrow. The same is true in business. Businesses that resist greening today due to a lack of information, a shortage of time, or limited political will may be the first to embrace it tomorrow as they see other businesses start the process and find success. Exceptional companies make change, and mediocre companies chase it. In this case, the exceptional companies are those that see the benefits of greening and have the guts to make positive changes even before their competitors do. Other companies will surely follow, but the spoils—media attention, impassioned employees, and a fatter bottom line—will go to the first to become green.

Green Culture Manifestations

Despite the frustratingly incomplete statistics for this new emerging green market, there are other indicators that point to the growth trend of all things green. Think of it—organic and natural food was a niche market until a mere decade ago, when the USDA launched their Organically Grown seal. Since then, the organic food market has grown at rates of approximately 20 percent each year, many times faster than the market for conventional food. Future growth is expected to continue at a high rate. Organic food has expanded from a small corner in neighborhood natural food stores to a commonplace feature in every major and minor grocery chain and big-box retailer.

In addition to food stores, most all other mainstream retailers, including big-box and department stores, have added green to their product offerings. In 2007, Home Depot began offering Eco Options in their stores, a specially labeled selection of 2,500 products meeting a predetermined list of green criteria that reduce negative environmental impacts. Wal-Mart, the largest retailer in the world, began to earnestly and vigorously green many different aspects of its business in 2005. The company taught employees to be green at work and at home through its Personal Sustainability Projects program. Wal-Mart began a green supply chain initiative to discover how more sustainable products could be made or bought by suppliers. The company began to require that suppliers use a green packaging rating system for products sold in their stores. This allows it to cut down the amount of packaging, use more renewable materials, and cut energy use. On top of everything else, Wal-Mart began selling organic food, sustainably raised seafood, and other green consumer products.

More evidence of green has found traction on our roads. Remember, automobiles were steadily increasing in size and gas guzzling capability until gas prices hit over $3 per gallon in the summer of 2006. By the summer of 2008, gas was more than four dollars per gallon, and smaller, energy-efficient cars started to be the darlings of the auto industy. SUVs and their large gas tanks were tanking. Small became synonymous with both gas savings and the ultimate in a hip style statement as seen in the robust sales of the Mini Cooper, Toyota Prius, and the very tiny Smart Car. The premium consumers paid for ultrahigh gas mileage cars started to make financial sense as the price of gas moved up. Drivers were also able make a patriotic and values statement with their car choice, showing off their green priorities of saving resources and reducing emissions as well as reducing dependence on foreign oil.

At the same time, green building became popular. High energy prices hit businesses in their building budgets. All energy costs were increasing rapidly including electricity for lighting, machinery, and air conditioning and natural gas for heating. This is expected to boost the new green building construction industry to $60 billion in revenue by 2010 according to McGraw-Hill's SmartMarket Trends Report 2008.

Another indication of the increasing cultural importance of green is revealed by where individuals and investment firms are putting their money. Socially responsible investing (SRI), which includes the universe of all things green, increased 324 percent from $639 billion in 1995 to $2.71 trillion in 2007 according to the 2007 SRI trends report in *The Green Money Journal*. Between 2005 and 2007, SRI assets increased more than six times the rate of all professionally managed assets. In 2007, nearly one in every nine dollars of professionally managed assets were involved in SRI. Socially responsible investing has moved from niche ethical player to mainstream.

Moreover, the American cultural bellwether, Hollywood, has also turned on the green spotlights. In 2007, Global Green held a pre–Oscar party, complete with green carpet and socially responsible, stunning stars, who helped with the rebuilding efforts in New Orleans after Hurricane Katrina. Every year in their April edition *Vanity Fair* magazine highlights green celebrities and activists. The issue has been touted as carbon neutral. Robert Redford, Julia Louis-Dreyfus, and Leonardo DiCaprio have all been highlighted in the magazine. Darryl Hannah has received many environmental awards and has an online blog on ecology as part of her website. Josh Hartnett drives a Prius. Hollywood celebrity Ed Begley Jr., an environmentalist since the 1960s, had a show first on HGTV and then on Planet Green, *Living with Ed*, where he lets viewers into his unorthodox extreme-green personal life in an effort to entertain and inform. In this day of reality TV and star imitation, as Hollywood goes so does Main Street America.

Even the travel sector has not been immune to green influences. Ecotourism, defined as responsible travel to natural areas without degrading the environment, is on the rise. It includes outdoor camping in remote areas, as well as luxurious eco-lodges and small ships that sail to hard-to-reach locales like Antarctica or the Galapagos Islands. Ecotourism also ensures that the money that travelers bring into the area stays local. This is no small phenomenon; ecotourism is growing three times faster than the tourism industry as a whole, according to a 2004 study by the International Ecotourism Society.

Add up the evidence on this recent proliferation of green in our culture and it is no wonder that some of the largest businesses in this country and the world are turning their time, attention, and capital to green. Initially, it occurred sporadically in a few business sectors, but now green is everywhere and impossible to ignore. In the next chapter, we will move from the overarching culture to business and organizations. You will learn how the concepts for green business evolved, and you will also be armed with more ammunition to convince you, your colleagues, and your suppliers that green business is the next revolution in the world of commerce. It is a revolution that you can't afford to miss, and it has already begun.

Chapter 3

The Green Business Zeitgeist

In 1992, I went to my first meeting of a national group that had recently formed, Business for Social Responsibility. I was amazed by the inspiring examples sitting around the table. CEOs like Anita Roddick from the Body Shop, Horst Rechelbacher, founder of Aveda, and Ben Cohen, cofounder of Ben & Jerry's ice cream, all talked about how their companies were making positive social change. Many had implemented programs to bring environmental responsibility to their products and services. Some used their product lines and advertising to advance social causes that they cared about, like world peace or ending poverty. Others had programs for employees that helped them live more balanced lives, including company-paid day care or progressive family-leave policies. Some had programs in the community, operating garden projects where the less fortunate could learn gardening skills and their children could escape the hot concrete of the city.

These CEOs were not competing on the basis of the size of their revenues or profits—the typical causes for corporate chest pounding. Instead they were competing on what they were doing with their businesses for the good of the community and the world. There was an undercurrent of belief in the possibility that business can and should be an agent for positive change and just might be the only thing capable of saving the world. The excitement and energy around these ideas at the early BSR conferences was absolutely intoxicating. I was instantly sold on the possibilities for my own businesses.

Business as Change Agent

The idea that business could be socially responsible was relatively new in the early 1990s. Similar to the terms green and sustainability, there was and has been no solid consensus about what social responsibility means. It was often defined in those early days as the golden rule—do unto others as you would have them do unto you. This applied to employees, the community, and the ecosystem where the businesses operated. Some defined social responsibility in business as just plain good business, because they believed that their success was attributable to treating all things well. The motto in those early years was that business could "do well by doing good."

Historically though, business had not been responsible for curing society's ills. This was the bailiwick of government and, for centuries before that, of organized religion. In fact, there are many economic theories that state companies have no business getting involved in social problems. The only purpose of business, according to this way of thinking, is to make money for the owners or stockholders. Anything beyond maximizing wealth is an unwelcome and unnecessary distraction.

Perhaps it was the influence of the Brundtland Commission's discussion of sustainable development as the means to a better world in the 1980s, but despite traditional economists' opinion of the purpose of business, companies began warming to this concept of change agent. Some business owners recognized that neither organized religion nor government had the power or the money any longer to fix the overwhelming problems in the world. Business did. Business also had an incentive: you can't sell widgets to someone who is starving or sick. And operating in a deteriorating environment puts raw material and energy access at risk. Gradually, business leaders began to understand that all of the adverse elements that were threatening society were also threatening their ability to make money. Some also understood that business was the only entity that had the money, power, and know-how to do something about it.

The socially responsible business movement took off in the United States in 1992, when business leaders formed the very visible Business for Social Responsibility nonprofit organization. The socially responsible business movement is also known as ethical business, conscious commerce, and corporate social responsibility.

According to Joel Makower's 1994 book, *Beyond the Bottom Line,* socially responsible business has several fundamental beliefs or principles.

> Employees are the most productive when they are engaged in meaningful work for a fair wage in a healthy working environment, are respected, and have a say in how they do their jobs.

> Companies are the most profitable over the long run when they are located in healthy communities with a pool of qualified workers, adequate education, and low crime rates.

> Companies function best when they treat the natural environment with care through minimizing waste, using resources efficiently, and treating nature with respect.

> Companies must look into the future and make decisions based on longer periods of time than quarterly earnings statements, which tend to skew the real costs of doing business (like not taking into account the effects of polluting a river or spewing greenhouse gases into the air).

> Corporate reputations will become more and more important as a legitimate product and service differentiator, separating the responsible companies from those that are not considered responsible.

The implication of these beliefs for companies that wanted to be socially responsible was that companies had to compete on a new level to attract and keep customers. It was no longer good enough to be in compliance with environmental laws. Instead, companies must go beyond compliance to protect the environment. Likewise, it was no longer acceptable to allow child labor in countries just because the local law didn't forbid it. The socially responsible business ethic mandated that companies make sure their factories were complying with their own behavior codes for operations.

The concept of sustainable development was honed and implemented by governments and nonprofit organizations around the world at the same time the social responsibility movement was being adopted by business. In practice, the two concepts are remarkably similar. Sustainable development is also concerned with the good of the environment, the community, and the economy. All three elements need to successfully work together when developing solutions to local or worldwide problems. Economies cannot stall when fixing environmental problems. Likewise, people and communities must be considered when dealing with economic development. In other words, business—the engine that was driving economic activity and historically had been part of both social and environmental problems—suddenly needed to be a part of the solution.

This intersection of sustainable development and socially responsible business in the early 1990s birthed the green business movement. Some wonks would probably say that green is a subset or only part of the concept of a socially responsible business or sustainability. But for me, a green business practitioner, a healthy planet is just as important as healthy communities and people. The economy, planet, and people are all inextricably connected. You can't have one without the other two. In this book, I will use *green business* interchangeably with *social responsibility*, *sustainability*, and *environmentally friendly*.

How do you quantify all these concepts? Some suggest using a triple bottom line. The term was coined by John Elkington in 1994 and expanded upon in his 1998 book, *Cannibals with Forks: The Triple Bottom Line of 21st Century Business*. The triple bottom line attempts to express social responsibility or sustainability in a profit/loss statement format for a business, proving that it isn't just some high-minded, impractical idea. The elements of the triple bottom line are the same as that for sustainability: social, environmental, and economic, or "people, profit, and planet" as it is characterized by SustainAbility for Shell, the oil company. It accounts for these elements through a "full cost" accounting method that quantifies, to some extent, the life cycle costs and their effect on natural capital (the environment) and human capital (the work force).

Implementing a system of accounting like the triple bottom line can seem a bit overwhelming at first, because it is a big change not only in how you perceive your world but in how you account for expenses. You must now factor in the cost of polluting or components of a carbon footprint. Institutions like banks and the IRS don't yet recognize this kind of accounting. Consumers don't either. But as standards and certifications for green products and services begin to incorporate some of these concepts and they become more widely available, methodologies like the triple bottom line or full-cost accounting will make more sense in the business world. For now, it is enough to know that such systems and standards exist. They provide another resource for you as you start on the greening journey. Measuring any kind of business progress is important, because in the world of organizations what gets measured gets accomplished.

It is undeniable that a shift in power and responsibility is underway on this planet. Global economics, life-threatening environmental issues like climate change and a growing world population with billions of people living in poverty, have created a new paradigm. For good or bad, business has ended up with the ability, the resources, and the incentive to fix the world's problems. This is what we, as twenty-first-century businesspeople, have signed up to do. Call it what you will—sustainability, social responsibility, ethical business, or conscious commerce—green business is a large part of the solution.

Small Business Equals Big Power

Perhaps you are thinking that this history and these concepts are interesting, but they don't apply to you because you own a small business and can't possibly make a difference in this overwhelming world. Well, it is time to wake up and feel your power. According to the U.S. Small Business Administration, small businesses make up 99 percent of all businesses nationwide, employ 50.6 percent of the non-farm private sector workforce, and are responsible for half the country's economic output. Small business has mighty power. A small organization is actually in a better position to implement green programs than many big ones because small businesses are more agile and able to quickly respond to changing market conditions. Smaller businesses also don't have as much at risk as large businesses when they make a big change. They don't have as many eyes watching for a mistake. A small business has the luxury of being able to experiment with change without being answerable to a big crowd of shareholders.

Success in greening a business depends on getting as many stakeholders (employees, customers, subcontractors, and owners) involved as possible. A small business starts this process with a natural advantage, since it has fewer people to convince and train. The results can be more quickly realized, making it easier to chart progress, which in turn will help everyone stay with the greening process.

The decision chain is shorter in a smaller organization, making it easier to implement anything the company wants to try without getting bogged down in bureaucracy. If you want to change a product formulation to make it less toxic or buy a more energy-efficient company vehicle, the company leadership can make a decision quickly. If it ends up being a bad decision, it is easy to reverse it. Much of the process of greening an organization is experimenting with what works and what doesn't. That is what makes it a creative process.

Small businesses don't have the marketing budgets of large businesses, but they do typically have a more intimate connection with their customers. This makes it possible to educate each customer more effectively about the company's green initiatives, raising their awareness and getting their agreement. Large companies can be more often accused of greenwashing, (phony or overstated greening), because they have to educate their consumers in a less-personal way through mass advertising.

It isn't all rosy of course. A small business may run into funding or expertise barriers when it comes to gaining approval for an environmental management certification program like ISO 14000 Series (International Standards Development) or the U.S. Green Building Council's LEED program for buildings. These types of programs are often geared toward large business because they are expensive, time consuming, and require professionals to oversee the program's start-up and ongoing progress. As green becomes more mainstream in the business world, more programs will cater to small business. Until then, there is nothing wrong with checking out the requirements of the existing programs and working toward complying, without officially paying for and receiving the certification. You will still be making strides to green your operation even if you don't have the certificate that proves it. One day, when either you can afford the program or another less-expensive program is in place, you will be ready.

Green Businesswomen

Women-owned or run companies may have a special gift when it comes to greening. Women have been in the forefront of environmental problem solving for decades. Dr. Ellen Swallow Richards was the first woman professional chemist back in the nineteenth century. She is credited with promoting the idea that people could affect the environment, either negatively or positively. Likewise, she argued, the environment could affect people (an idea that was not widely accepted for another hundred years). This led to the development of ecology as a field of study. Rachel Carson (discussed in the last chapter), the founder of the modern-day environmental movement, was a notable female green pioneer. Gro Harlem Brundtland, the female head of the Brundtland Commission, popularized sustainable development.

Likewise, women have often been environmental grassroots activists. Remember Erin Brokovich, who took on big business over a cancer cluster near her home and won? Or Lois Gibbs, who led the effort in the 1970s to move families away from Love Canal, a chemical waste dump site? These were women who feared for their families and community and did something to stop the problem.

There have also been countless successful pioneering female green business owners like Anita Roderick of the Body Shop, Nell Newman of Newman's Own Organics, and Monica Nassif, founder and CEO of Caldrea Company, an upscale green cleaning products company. I could name dozens of other women in this group of business leaders who took the green plunge long before it was safe or fashionable.

There are good reasons why women excel at green. This is not to say that men are not capable of it—they certainly are, and in fact there is a long list of male environmental heroes. But having environmental awareness and concern may come more naturally to women. Studies by the Institute for Women's Policy Research point to a higher level of concern in women over environmental risks. Women innately understand an ecosystem; after all, each woman is an ecosystem for her offspring. Anything positive or negative that a woman does to her body before or during pregnancy can affect the future for her offspring. Collaboration and holistic thinking are two of the hallmarks of green. The idea that everything is connected and that we need to work through issues collaboratively are concepts that women intuitively understand and frequently use in solving problems.

For the same reasons previously described, much of the innovation in the world happens in small businesses. Small businesses may not have easy access to capital, but they have something more useful: guts and determination. For the past two decades, according to the Center for Women's Business Research, women have been growing their 10.4 million businesses two times faster than men. Women-owned businesses employ nearly 13 million people and generate $1.9 trillion in sales. The center has also carried out studies on the characteristics of women business owners and found them to be risk takers as well as relationship builders. Combine all of this with the fact that women have a knack for green and it is extremely likely that there will be a proliferation of green businesses over the next few decades led by women entrepreneurs.

A Green Tipping Point

For both men and women entrepreneurs, there is no business without the consumer. Some complain that consumers are not demanding green in sufficient numbers to push forward green business. There is a green market, but is there a big enough consumer outcry for green products or services? In Europe and many other parts of the developed world, consumers are demanding green. In the United States, business sometimes seems to be producing green products they are not sure consumers are ready to buy.

Companies that dwell on this lack of consumer motivation may be caught with their green pants down around their knees. Things are changing due to the increase in consumer education, understanding, and perception about subjects such as the climate crisis. In a study the spring of 2008, Havas Media found that 79 percent of consumers in the United Kingdom, United States, Mexico, Brazil, Germany, and France said they would rather buy from companies doing their best to reduce their environmental impact. Eighty-nine percent said that they are likely to buy more green goods in the next twelve months. The study also found that people are looking to business for solutions rather than to their governments. This is good news for companies that have begun the greening process.

Be assured: the time has come. We are close to achieving critical mass of green awareness in both consumers and businesspeople in this country. Once we reach this heightened green awareness, good environmental practices will no longer be optional for organizations. Green will determine whether a brand image is good or tarnished, resulting in strong or weak market share. You need to be ready, not tardy to the green business party.

Green Business Manifestations

So far there are no studies that indicate the number of businesses that are going green. There are some books on the subject, plenty of web resources, and even some periodicals that discuss various green initiatives in which businesses engage. But even in the absence of empirical data, we can see the depth and breadth of the green business trend when we look at the current list of companies from nearly every sector in the economy that are exhibiting some green behavior. Coke bought Odwalla, and Pepsi bought Naked Juice, both health- and natural-oriented juice drinks. Traditional chemical cleaning companies are beginning to sell less-toxic product options, like Green Works from Clorox. Petroleum companies are investing in and developing renewable energy technologies. The übercorporate giant, G.E., has its Ecomagination initiative that provides innovative solutions to environmental challenges. Other highly publicized examples of the green business zeitgeist include the elimination of clamshell packaging by McDonald's, Wal-Mart's commitment to greening everything including the corporate kitchen sink, and FedEx's fleet of hybrid delivery trucks.

According to *The Innovations Review 2008: Making* Green *the New Business as Usual*, a 2008 report from the Environmental Defense Fund, environmental sustainability efforts are creating new markets, providing competitive advantages, and saving companies millions of dollars. The report was a first of its kind, using best practices to feature green business solutions that could be used as a model for other businesses across industry sectors. The report highlighted successful company initiatives from the likes of Patagonia, Ikea, Nike, Hewlett-Packard, and Yahoo!. Since 2002, Sun Microsystems has reduced greenhouse gases by 20 percent through energy-saving computer chips and allowing employees to telecommute. They have also saved millions of dollars in fuel costs and office space.

It is not all giant multinational corporations that are leading the movement either. Small and medium-sized companies are also greening, but often not in such a visible way. Hundreds of online green businesses are hawking their wares to the environmentally inclined consumer. Organic food markets are cropping up in shopping areas of big cities and small towns across the country. Thousands of small, natural personal-care product companies are making nontoxic soaps, shampoos, and lotions. Dry-cleaning operations that use less-toxic cleaning solutions can be found in most locales. Small retail stores are catering to customers smitten by low-impact, clean, or green clothing. Even farming businesses are getting into the green act, turning pig dung into electricity and leasing land for wind turbines. Every industry, business sector, and market has been touched by this green business phenomenon.

Another indication of the green business movement momentum is the new class of employee, the green-collar worker. She or he is a blue-collar worker doing a job that has an environmentally friendly bent to it. Erecting wind turbines, distilling biofuels and bioplastics, building green buildings, and installing solar panels are all examples of green-collar jobs. Elected officials have begun to compete for green investment to attract government green-collar jobs. Many view green-collar jobs as a way to add new jobs to the American economy.

The broader term for the entire movement encompassing green-collar jobs, clean and renewable technologies, and all aspects of green business is the green economy. Some experts say that the green economy will be so large and ubiquitous that it will eclipse the world-changing Industrial Revolution in the history books of the future.

Consider the fact that in the early 1990s business concern about environmental issues and sustainability was only taken seriously by a few smaller companies. Today, the concern and the corresponding action stretch from Wall Street to Main Street. It's time to get on board. Now that you have a good understanding of what green means and why to green, the next two sections of the book will give you the tools to begin and expand green initiatives in your own organization.

Part II

How Do I Care
The Office, Factory, or Warehouse

Chapter 4

Greening the Inside Space I— Maintaining Green

Greening your building maintenance is a no-brainer, and it's a good way to get started greening your business. Most of the strategies are fairly simple to implement and many are no or low cost. The benefits are tangible:

> It gives you a sense of control over your indoor environment

> It saves money

> It makes your workers healthier, happier, and more productive

As employees become more sophisticated about greening their own homes, they are beginning to expect it at work. They consider things like good indoor air quality a workplace right. How we choose to clean and maintain our buildings can determine if our air is good or bad.

Rising Energy Costs

Another reason to green your maintenance is that as utility costs increase and global warming becomes more of a threat, it makes more and more sense to aggressively pursue energy conservation and efficiency. Barry Bannister, an analyst with the brokerage and investment firm Stifel Nicolaus, recently forecast that fuel costs will raise retail electric rates 69 percent by 2015 largely due to the increasing price of coal. That is more than double the increase of the past ten years. Our physical space is a natural starting point for these changes. That is why a growing number of business owners are becoming aware of how to maintain their physical space using green practices.

Green property management or green building maintenance means using human-healthy and planet-friendly maintenance products, procedures, and equipment in any kind of building or office to ensure the health of the occupants and the protection of the natural environment.

Green building maintenance can be achieved on a scale ranging from millions of square feet, where facilities management is centrally controlled by a company division, down to a sole proprietor's home office. The type of property that houses your business (store, factory, or office) will determine which green practices will give you the most bang for your buck or comfort for the trouble. But a building is a building. All buildings have a shell, are heated or cooled, need to be cleaned, and provide a working environment for the occupants. Regardless of the size or use of the structure, the benefits of greening maintenance are the same:

> Trimming expenses

> Protecting the outdoors from effluents (water, air, and soil)

> Keeping the people inside safe and happy

There are many opportunities to engage the building staff by switching to the new sustainable products and practices in this age of green building. But many facilities management people give up and go back to the way they've always done it because change can be tough. So remember that the key to making lasting improvements is changing behavior and expectations and not just using the latest green maintenance invention. The most successful programs train and retrain building staff and occupants over and over. It is continuous improvement, not sudden change, that produces success.

Opportunity: Detox Your Space

Green Cleaning

Most working Americans toil away in some kind of man-made structure for eight to twelve hours a day, five days a week, fifty weeks a year. One-quarter to one-third of our day is spent in a building that, more likely than not, has dirtier air inside than out. According to the EPA, indoor air can be many times more polluted than outdoor air. Dirty indoor air at its worst can lead to worker sickness and absenteeism. But even mildly poor indoor air quality can lead to headaches and a worker malady known as sick building syndrome.

Fortunately, fixing indoor air quality is usually inexpensive and involves making some simple choices. The first step to making improvements is to be aware that building practices can affect indoor air.

As asthma and cancer rates have risen, we have become steadily more aware of the chemicals contained in our cleaning products at home, yet we don't often know or care about what kind of products are used in our work environments. Part of the reason is that the cleaning staff is never seen. They do their cleaning and straightening while most of us are asleep. We are only reminded of these cleaning angels if something is left dirty or a mess happens during the day. Cleaners are often unappreciated by other staff members, so it is no wonder that the products they use are not typically considered an integral part of a green building maintenance plan.

The truth is that the cleaning crew is typically cleaning with heavy-duty toxic chemicals, and they are probably at risk for having health-related issues as they age. Depending on the types of chemicals they use to clean the bathrooms, the floors, and surfaces of our spaces, we may be compromising our own health and that of our staff.

There are strong environmental reasons to consider as well:

> Commercial cleaning is a chemical-intensive industry that literally goes down the drain and has a negative impact on our water supply.

> Most cleaning chemicals are made from petroleum and use a tremendous amount of raw materials and energy to produce.

> Toxic cleaning supplies create disposal problems at the end of their life.

All these are compelling reasons to switch to green cleaning. An easy fix is to purchase green cleaning products or insist that your cleaning company use less-toxic cleaning products. Such products are widely available today, and their efficacy has improved to rival traditional products. Another perk is that they have become price competitive with traditional, chemical-laden products. They are made from enzymes, natural compounds, and most often are produced from plants rather than petroleum. These green cleaning products are typically sold in concentrates, which is an environmental plus because it takes less energy for the manufacturer to transport the product without the water premixed into it—more bottles fit on a truck or train. They are less toxic so they are less harmful to the cleaning staff and building occupants. And there is no need for a trip to a hazardous waste facility when the products are finished.

Contrary to green cleaning purists, it has been my experience that occasionally a toxic chemical cleaner is the only product that will do a specific job—like getting a tough stain out. So it is important to train the cleaning staff to start with the least toxic product first and then move up the toxicity chain to find the one that does the job for that particular situation. Rather than starting with the most toxic product in your janitor closet, always start with the least toxic. Remember the ultimate goal is to reduce toxic chemical use.

There are no universally recognized labeling requirements for green cleaning products yet, but there are several product certification programs that can help you sort through various green cleaning product and equipment options. The Green Seal (*www.greenseal.org*) and Environmental Choice (*www.ecologo.org*) websites provide specific product names that they certify as environmentally sound. These programs have established standards that a product must meet in order to be certified, including efficacy—working as well or better than other products in its class—and testing of the environmental claim.

Control Pests Naturally

In a perfect world, we would accept pests as part of our environment. After all, they were here first, and maybe we should learn to peacefully coexist with a few spiders or ants in our indoor space. In reality, we just don't feel warm and fuzzy at the sight of an army of ants in the lobby, bats in the belfry, or cockroaches in the kitchen—not to mention the health hazard this poses. The challenge is finding a system to deal with pests that doesn't poison every other living thing in the building and taint our indoor air.

Fortunately, such a solution exists: integrated pest management (IPM). IPM is also known as the barrier method, not because it keeps mice from getting pregnant but because it stops mice (and all other rodents and bugs) from entering the building in the first place. Periodically inspect the entire building envelope for entry points and seal them closed. Some managers of buildings would call it good old common sense to check the building exterior from ground to roof several times a year, instead of spraying the building inside and out with a toxic insecticide.

If pests have already gotten a ride into the building via a delivered package, a person, or by walking (or crawling) through the front door, IPM suggests eliminating all food and drink for the little buggers. This means that a maintenance person must inspect the inside of the building for leaking pipes, messy garbage, and dripping faucets. If reducing food sources doesn't work, the next step is to use the least toxic product available to eliminate pest reproduction and eventually snuff them out of existence (at least as far as your building is concerned). This may involve mechanical traps or less-toxic pesticides. The rule with all green building practices is—less is more. Similar to green cleaning products, use the least toxic practice first, and if that doesn't work move toward more toxic. Never start with a toxic bomb when a small bit of caulk might do the trick.

Almost every community in the country has an IPM pest control company these days. It's best to do some research online. Another source for less toxic pest control is your local university. Universities that have agriculture or horticulture programs often have up-to-date information about local IPM solutions and sources. Once you get an IPM program going, long-term costs should be reduced, because you are eliminating a regular pesticide-spraying program. The dollars saved with IPM may initially be invested in sealing up the building or improved sanitation, but these are dollars well spent. In the long run, IPM practices can even add value to the real estate because the final result is an improved building.

Freshen the Air

Most buildings have stale or smelly air at least some of the time. It may be cooking odors from a restaurant or cafeteria, bathroom smells, or an old moldy moisture problem, but it's there. The most common toxic solution for building odors is the cover-up. Companies use a wall-mounted gizmo that I call a stink-spritzer to automatically spray a chemical fragrance into the space so that the bad smell is masked with a heavier, more acceptable smell. Now, if you think this doesn't seem like a good way to solve a problem, you are right—it is deception. We certainly don't want to get into trouble with our building occupants by covering up a problem with a different problem. Most chemical air fresheners contain endocrine-disrupting, hazardous chemicals known as phthalates. Phthalates are often not named on a contents label, which instead uses the word "fragrance." This kind of smell killer is not good for anybody, and people with lung conditions like asthma may be especially sensitive to chemical fragrance.

A better way to deal with a stinky situation is to identify the problem. If the odor is caused by moisture or a leak, remove and replace damaged building materials within forty-eight hours of the water intrusion or as soon as the smell is detected. The odor should then disappear. If the smell is an ongoing problem—from a bathroom or kitchen area, for example—first make sure that the room is well ventilated with fans that remove stale air to the outside. If that doesn't work, consider installing an air purification system centrally for the entire building or locally in the affected area only. Be sure to avoid air purifiers with ozone systems. Ozone is good in the sky but at ground level is poisonous and can be harmful to breathe.

Another way to remove odors is to use a mineral derived from volcanic ash called zeolite. Zeolite absorbs odors naturally. It can be "recharged" at no cost by letting it sit in sunlight for several hours to release absorbed contaminants. Zeolite is sometimes found in air purifiers as part of the filtering system. You can purchase it in mesh pouches that can be hidden in a room, allowing it to do its work without using any toxic chemicals.

Believe it or not, common houseplants can also help cleanse your indoor air. Plants absorb carbon dioxide that humans exhaust through breathing, and they produce oxygen, which we need to feel good and think clearly. Plants are natural air cleaners and can absorb airborne toxins. Common spider plants and azaleas are champion air cleaners. Strategically placing plants through out a working environment can purify the air, increase humidity in the winter, and provide a splash of green, which can help lift the spirits in any building. A NASA study suggests that for plants to be effective as air cleaners there should be one large plant for every 100 feet of space. But be careful not to overwater the plants or they could develop a mold problem, harming, instead of helping, your indoor air quality.

Opportunity: Energy Savings

Energy prices are higher than they have ever been. Gone are the days of "penny cheap power" from the utilities. Yes, we all know that saving resources saves money, and it rings especially true today. Gasoline prices and electricity and natural gas rates have hit all-time highs, and there is no downward trend in sight. As we come to the end of the carbon era and search for cheaper renewable sources of energy, we are in for an unpredictable and crazy transitional period that will make it difficult for business to plan and budget. So it is now more important than ever to pay attention to how your firm is using and wasting energy.

Energy Use in Offices

30 percent	Lighting
25 percent	Space Heating
16 percent	Office Equipment
9 percent	Water Heating
9 percent	Space Cooling
11 percent	Other

Source: Derived from the Commercial Buildings Energy Consumption Survey (CBECS) 1995, released July 1998 by the Energy Information Administration.

You've heard it many times: the United States has less than 5 percent of the world's population yet uses 25 percent of the world's energy. Nonresidential buildings account for 30–40 percent of this energy use. So there is tremendous opportunity to reduce use, save money, and make our building budgets more predictable.

The resistance to doing something expensive is understandable, but greening need not be expensive. Sometimes simple things make the biggest impact. That is doubly true when it comes to saving energy. The benefits are simple: savings in energy used, less money spent on utilities, and fewer carbon emissions. All companies should immediately take the following low-cost and no-cost steps:

Adjust your thermostat—Set it to sixty-eight degrees in the winter, fifty-five degrees at night, and seventy-five degrees in the summer with a relative humidity of no more than 55 percent. Avoid heating and cooling at the same time. Install programmable thermostats in each heating and cooling zone. Once set, cover and lock all thermostats. You may get a few whiners, but you always did no matter what the temperature setting and you will be doing the right thing for the planet and your bottom line.

Maintain air flow—Do a walk around and unblock all heating and cooling registers. Sounds too elementary to be true, but furniture or equipment is often set in front of or on top of vents. Have maintenance check for leaky ductwork and seal it. Regularly clean and disinfect drain pans in heating and cooling equipment. Make sure that furnace filters are on a schedule to be changed monthly or bimonthly. You would be surprised how often a busy maintenance staff overlooks these simple service items.

Start a daytime cleaning program—Look at any downtown business district at 10:00 p.m. and you will see the buildings lit up like they are occupied with workers. The truth is that the lights in the entire building are on for a couple of cleaning crews or advertising by the building owners. Start a new trend and request that the building be cleaned during business hours while all occupants are working. Have all lights turn off in the building through a policy or timer by a reasonable early evening time when most of the workers have gone home. This kind of policy also has the unexpected benefit of killing fewer birds that are attracted to lighted buildings at night during the spring and fall migration seasons.

Stop vampire loads—A "phantom load" or passive electric use is caused by electronics that are plugged in and turned off but continue to drain electricity. (By the way, screen savers are not an energy-saving device.) Develop a policy that all equipment must be plugged into power strips that are turned off at quitting time or when not in use for two hours. This can be written into a company policy manual.

A typical desktop computer uses 65 to 250 watts (refer to the owners manual or contact the manufacturer for the exact number). Add 35 to 80 more watts for a monitor. Keep in mind that different computers and monitors use different amounts of watts. You can calculate the cost of running each computer in your business with this formula: (watts x hours used divided by 1,000) x cost per kilowatt hour = total cost for whatever period you are measuring (a month or year). For example, assuming a $.13 per kilowatt hour, a typical PC in a business running twenty-four hours per day with a seventeen-inch LCD monitor will cost around $93 per year. The same equipment running only eight hours per day will cost $40 per year.

Improved Lighting

Lights in a commercial building are the biggest user of electricity of all building equipment, and much of it is wasted electricity because lighting systems are often outdated or poorly designed. There are few buildings that couldn't benefit from improved lighting. Most buildings are overlit in some areas and underlit in others. And some buildings, like retail operations that need well-lit displays to sell their product, have hot spots that can overheat people and equipment.

There are some very common-sense improvements that can be made easily and on the cheap.

1.   Take an inventory to make sure lighting is located where the light is needed. In an office, desks and work surfaces need to be well lit. In a factory, equipment areas need to have a higher concentration of light. In a store, merchandise needs to be highlighted. Don't waste electricity by lighting entire rooms when a separate switch can turn on task lights where you need it, when you need it. Lighting reflective colors, rather than dark paint on ceilings, can also give you more light without increasing power use.

2.   If a light is on and no one sees it, is it still on? Yes. Don't waste electricity in any unoccupied space. For little money, you can install occupancy sensors in rooms that are only used periodically, like bathrooms or storerooms. Develop a policy that lights will not be turned on if a space is well lit from daylight through windows or skylights. It always surprises me when my staff has blinds closed and their lights on or when an empty room with a light switch is always on.

3.   Set up a committee to monitor and do periodic checking on the use of lights. It may sound like too much micromanaging, but encouraging the proper use of lighting through reminders, policies, and policing is a low-cost way to save energy and money. Once your staff understands your green motives, they will likely enjoy making their own difference by following through on your new light-use policy.

The next level in greening your lighting is a full or partial retrofit. This means replacing current lighting with energy-saving lighting options. The cost and payback period for a retrofit is becoming more worthwhile all the time as electricity costs increase. The majority of retrofits have a two- to five-year payback period (in other words, whatever the cost of the project, you will get it back in energy savings in that period of time), which will get even shorter as electricity rates climb. The cost of the retrofit will depend on the condition of your current wiring and electrical system. How accessible your wiring and fixtures are to an electrician trying to install the new equipment will raise or lower costs. There are many electricians and lighting specialty companies that will review your current system and give you a retrofit plan and bid complete with an estimated payback period for the entire cost of the project. Retrofits include use of compact fluorescent bulbs and newer fluorescent tubes with longer-lasting ballasts and the newer LED lighting technologies that produce less heat. In fact, by 2012–2014 new federal energy efficiency standards will apply to all light bulbs requiring bulbs to use 25 percent to 30 percent less energy than today's bulbs. Unable to meet the standard, the typical 40–100 watt incandescent bulbs will be phased out.

Tune Up Heating and Cooling Systems

No one loves to talk HVAC (heating, ventilating, and cooling) unless they are building engineers, architects, or energy wonks. Never fear. It is really very simple—comfort is the goal. But comfort comes at a price to an organization and the environment. So the easiest and least costly thing that any organization through its maintenance staff can do is maintain its HVAC equipment properly.

> Change filters monthly and more often if the building is dusty or dirty.

> Clean the condenser coils at the beginning and end of every season.

> Regularly and often check, clean, and disinfect condensation pans so bacteria doesn't build up (the culprit in the original Legionnaires' disease outbreak).

> Check and recheck HVAC controls continuously so that the correct amount of outside air is brought in—not too much and not too little.

> Chart and monitor heating and cooling utility bills for unusual non-weather-related variations to help spot equipment inefficiencies.

> The most well-run buildings provide maintenance staff and managers with policies and checklists for all HVAC building systems.

It is also possible to get a building "commissioned" or "recommissioned." The process is similar to hiring an expert to do an energy audit in your home. The key is to hire an expert you can trust. Hire an independent expert or engineer to go through the building systems to make sure the systems are running properly and make recommendations for improvement in the HVAC system. This is a relatively inexpensive process and can result in energy bill savings that can be quantified before you spend money on improvements. When it is time to replace HVAC equipment, be sure to purchase high-efficiency equipment and high-performance motors.

Easy Steps to Green

Following are seven helpful tips for implementing green maintenance in your building. If you can achieve all that this chapter suggests, you can save as much as 5–25 percent on your utility bills. You will also likely have a happier, more productive, and healthier staff resulting in further improvements to your bottom line.

1. Take an Inventory of What You Have Done Already

Most likely, your building has already accomplished at least a couple of the suggestions in this chapter. Use the maintenance checklist at the back of the book to find out where you are currently and see how far you need to go. At the very least, it will make you feel as though you have already made some green progress. Keep in mind that green is a journey, not a destination, and all companies have room for improvement.

2. Build a Team to Develop and Implement a Plan to Be Greener

Appoint someone from the cleaning crew or cleaning company, the maintenance staff, a building or plant manager, several building occupants, and someone from management to sit on a committee that will develop a plan for implementing a green building maintenance program. You will need to find local experts, vendors, and products for some of the changes. Other changes will require development of a policy or a change in policy so it is important to have the key players involved at the start of the process

Typically, it is easy to get employees to volunteer for this kind of committee once the company has made a commitment to green. The committee can meet during business hours and be an integral part of the operation with goals of reducing resource use and cutting costs. Vendors of green products or services will often come to a planning meeting to help you sort through options.

3. Select a Test Area or Building

Don't go hog wild and change everything at once. You will frustrate everyone. Start with a test floor of rooms or a test building. Don't change everything all at once. Phase in the changes. Be sure to plan carefully for the test area because a successful test will help keep the momentum building for a full implementation.

4. Identify a Baseline

Collect baseline information from various related functions within the company or building. Record a year of utility bills. Get cleaning product, pest control, and air-freshening costs. Take an inventory of lights on and off. Develop a comfort survey for occupants asking questions about temperature and other indoor comfort issues (see the example survey in Appendix B). Find out the average number of sick days for employees. Once you have a baseline, you can more clearly prove the merits of the program as you enter implementation.

5. Train the Staff

Training and retraining staff is a continuous process when changing the way things are done in any business. But in green building maintenance it is critical that the staff understands both how to make the change and why they are making it. For example, sometimes when switching to less-toxic cleaning products, cleaning staff will be bothered by the lack of smell of the product and try to use more of it as a result. They need to be shown that the toxic smell isn't good for them and isn't what creates the clean surface.

6. Communicate Changes to Occupants

As with every green improvement, shout it from the top of the building. Let occupants know about the green changes you are making and why. With the heightened awareness of all things green, most of your company's employees will cut you some slack if things don't go exactly right. On the flip side, if green transitions are making life better for workers, they need to know that too. You will have gained some bragging rights!

7. Evaluate and Tweak As You Go

Once you have made some of the changes, look at the numbers to verify that you are making progress. Request utility bills and compare old with new after the changes. Track employee complaints and absenteeism to see if the green practices are having a positive affect on comfort and health. If progress is being made, then celebrate it in your green team and in the broader business. If progress has yet to be realized, tweak the program to get more cooperation from staff and occupants. The most bang for your trouble will be realized when all forces—occupants, staff, managers, and customers—are moving in the same green direction.

Chapter 5

Greening the Inside Space II— Building or Remodeling Green

In 1995, my company was one of the first in our region to build a green office building. It was a crazy idea back then, because easily accessible information about how to construct an office building in an environmentally friendly way did not exist. The term green building hadn't been coined. In fact, our low-tech, modest foray into this territory was so unique at the time, some considered it bizarre. Luckily, our state's pollution control agency saw things differently and cited our building as an model example of pollution reduction. We received media attention from around the country. As the instigator of the project and owner of the business, I was called everything from a treehugger (in a supposedly derogatory way) to a revolutionary (in the good sense—at least that's what I chose to believe).

We started with an existing building and took it apart nail by nail, donating many components for reuse. We then rebuilt it, using certified sustainable wood, nontoxic paints and adhesives, energy-efficient lighting, carpeting made from old plastic pop bottles, and a state-of-the-art air purification system. Our costs of building green were about 10 percent over that of traditional construction. As we had planned, we were quickly able to recoup that extra capital expenditure in savings with lower utility costs, a rise in productivity, and less employee turnover.

Our motivation for wanting to build green was simple: Our lease was running out, and to further our green initiative we bought a building and turned it green. Greening our physical space seemed to be the next natural level in our company's green evolution. We weren't sure what greening our physical space involved, but we forged ahead anyway, sorting through the few green products and vendors that were available and learning as we went.

It was tough going. We couldn't find a contractor that was willing to do the green things that we wanted, so my maintenance and construction company took on the project, armed with only the desire to build green. We had no roadmap.

Today *green building* has become a catchall to describe just about anything earth friendly that you can do to a building and the property around it. But true green building is a holistic approach to building as a living system, incorporating some or all of such components as:

> Energy efficiency

> Indoor air quality

> Resource efficiency

> Sustainable landscaping

> Waste reduction

> Toxics reduction

> Smart growth

Authentic green building also makes use of local materials and a site design that is mindful of sun and weather exposure. Don't be confused when green building is referred to as green design, high-performance building, energy efficient, sustainably built or designed, eco-friendly, or consciously built—it is all green building or some subset of it.

Green is showing up everywhere in real estate circles these days. CB Richard Ellis Group announced plans to be carbon neutral in its own operations by 2010. The Merchandise Mart in Chicago, the largest commercial building in the world, received its LEED Silver certification from the U.S. Green Building Council. A fall 2007 report by RREEF, the San Francisco real estate investment advisor, warns that demand will eventually strongly favor green buildings, so property owners need to quickly adapt or risk owning property with obsolete building choices.

But not everyone is a convert. Even though green building is all the rage, there are still some lingering myths I would like to dispel.

Green buildings are only for big companies with deep pockets. Yes, the early adopters of anything are mostly the wealthy, because they can afford to fool around with what others might consider experimental. Also keep in mind that we hear about sexy upscale properties first because the media focuses on them. Imagine if Lindsay Lohan were to build a green building—need I say more. The reality is that green buildings make economic sense for both large and small business. The savings can improve bottom lines for any size organization.

Earth friendly equals ugly. Banish the thoughts of earth shelter buildings and geodesic dome structures—bad ideas from the seventies (remember leisure suits were once "in" too). These days, earth friendly cannot be distinguished from the rest of the buildings in a neighborhood. Some of the most fabulously beautiful building materials available are green. For example, in green kitchens you'll find counters and backsplashes with gem-colored recycled glass tiles. Or look for natural, funky-colored Marmoleum or stained concrete floors. And don't forget less-toxic paints in all colors and natural, earth-type plaster applications for walls. All are gracing the pages of the most chic decorating magazines. Earth friendly can equal stylish, hip, and beautiful design.

Green building is a fad that won't last. Nothing could be further from the truth. Anyone with common sense can see that the entire real estate business is going through violent change over high operating costs. Europe has long experienced high resource cost, and Europeans have used green building strategies for decades. It has never been considered a fad in Europe, and it won't be a passing fancy here either. Designing for efficiency is not a new concept but one whose time has come, as energy and water costs go through the roof in this country. Green building technologies will be the only way that buildings will be built affordably in the future.

Economic Benefits of Greening an Existing Building

Increases productivity by as much as 10 percent

Increases job satisfaction by as much as 24 percent

Reduces absenteeism by as much as 45 percent

Lowers utility costs by as much as 50 percent

Reduces life cycle costs by at least 25 percent

Source: U.S. Green Building Council website

You can easily find green building examples, case studies, products, certifications, and qualified professionals. There is much good information and help available for people who want to green a building or office space today. Many architects and design firms have become repositories of this information, but there is also an amazing amount of free information available on the web if you are greening on a budget or doing initial research (which is a good idea). A few easily accessible websites are *www.usgbc.org, www.rmi.org,* and *www.greenclips.com.* It is possible to do a low-budget, low-tech greening of a building or to take advantage of every new technology that exists and build an experimental cutting-edge, super-green building. But realize that it is your responsibility as the business owner to ask the architect, contractor, or design firm to incorporate green into the building. We are not yet at the point where professionals assume their clients want to go green. So you must ask.

Perhaps the most difficult thing about building green today is the number of options. It's hard to know how and where to start. This chapter is a quick primer on green building. It will help you understand the various broad options for building green, tell you where to find information, and help you begin greening your physical space when you want to make some substantial changes to your office suite or building.

Opportunity: Greening the Location and Site

While it is tempting to build new and green as a way to slow global warming, the truth is that the least expensive option may just be to stay put. It may be less glamorous to recycle your current space, but you will be greener for it. This is true whether you occupy a home office or millions of square feet.

If it is time to move because your lease is up or you have outgrown your current corporate digs, consider the options carefully before you jump to the first suburban outpost that will throw some money your way. Buying or leasing an existing building is the ultimate in recycling. A tremendous amount of energy and resources have already been expended building the current structure and retrofitting it to someone's needs. Rather than building new, it is almost always more earth friendly to buy used and remodel.

As you begin your search, look for a site that has easy access to public transportation so that employees can have a no-car option for getting to work. Consider locating to an infill lot or an existing building in an already developed area that is close to restaurants and shopping for employees. Reducing driving needs of employees garners green points. If you do build new from the ground up, check into building on a brownfield (a once-polluted site that has been cleaned and is available for reuse). The government sometimes offers incentives to develop a site that has been cleaned up or needs cleaning up. Such development performs a service to the neighborhood, because it uses land that has been a blighted spot for many years. At a minimum, build as near to where your workers live as possible to cut down on commuting energy, pollution, and travel time.

Opportunity: Resource Savings

One area that most business owners overlook when they are building or remodeling green is the reuse of old building components. It's fairly common these days to see a relatively new upscale office or retail building being gutted and everything from gorgeous lumber with an appealingly aged patina to shiny marble foyers tiles thrown into a dumpster. In fact, over 30 percent of landfills consist of construction and demolition waste. Finding an option other than bash and throw is an idea worth seriously considering. In the past several years, a new industry (or shall we say a really old industry)—salvage—has been born again. In this incarnation, it is called deconstruction or construction in reverse. It means taking an old building apart brick by brick in order to reuse, donate, or resell as many building components as possible. Under this arrangement, virtually nothing goes to a landfill. Now that's recycling.

Deconstructing for (Non)Profit

In some parts of the country, nonprofit organizations have been set up to manage deconstruction operations. If that is true in your area, it is not even necessary to have a general contractor willing to do the extra work. The nonprofit, which typically employs people who need work, will come and deconstruct the parts of the building that you want removed. The building owner then donates the deconstructed building components to the nonprofit. The building owner gets rid of the things she doesn't want and usually can claim a tax deduction. The nonprofit resells for a profit the building components that it removes. New jobs are created in the community, there is less debris for landfills, and fewer virgin resources have been used to make new products. It is a green win-win situation for everyone involved.

If you are building new from the ground up, be sure to make it a requirement in your contract with the contractor that he divert a large percentage of the construction waste from the landfill. A good rule of thumb is to ask that at least 50 percent of the waste not reach the landfill, but, of course, the more diverted waste the better. Alternatives to landfilling construction waste include re-use of salvageable materials like wood and marble flooring in a new structure or grinding up leftover drywall that hasn't been treated with fire resistant chemicals for use as a soil amendment.

Use recycled or recycled content materials in your new space. Anything that you purchase that is made from something that has been recycled results in three huge green benefits:

1.   It saves the material from the landfill

2.   It takes much less energy to make a product out of recycled materials than virgin materials, and any reduction in energy use helps fight global warming

3.   Unused virgin material resources such as oil, metal, or wood are conserved

Recycled content can be found in other building materials too. Many carpets now are made with recycled content. Some are made from old plastic soda bottles and others from previously used carpet that has been ground up and made into new carpet or carpet squares. Recycled or refurbished cubicles that look like new can be used in office build-outs. Other examples of building materials with recycled content are:

> Cellulose insulation (made from recycled wood fiber—primarily newspaper)

> Recycled plastic lumber

> Tiles made from recycled crushed glass

> Recycled content rubber for indoor walkways and elevators floors

The higher percentage of recycled content in a material, the more environmentally beneficial it is.

Another simple green resource idea is to purchase local building materials. Just as with buying food local, buying local building supplies cuts down on transportation, which is costly in energy use and emissions. If you are located in the northern half of the country, there are plenty of resources for locally grown wood. Look for both locally grown and sustainably harvested wood with a Forest Stewardship Council (FSC) certification and you will be using a resource that is as green as it can be.

It may seem that water is very plentiful in the United States, but more than 4.8 billion gallons each day are taken from surface water and aquifers to keep our toilets flushing in our homes and businesses. As water supplies become overburdened and fresh water becomes more expensive, there are some things that businesses can do to cut down on water usage in their bathrooms and inside facilities.

Older toilets use four to eight gallons of water for each flush. New toilets since the 1992 Energy Policy Act, which established some water conservation standards, have a maximum flush of 1.6 gallons—a much-improved flush. There have been further bathroom innovations in the past decade that exceed the 1992 requirements. Some of the more interesting include:

> Waterless urinals

> Dual-flush toilets (up for liquids, down for solids requiring more water)

> Composting toilets with no water

> Sensors for hands-free toilet flushing

> Touch-free hand washing and drying, like those found at major
  airports around the country

All of these innovations decrease the amount that goes into
the sewer system as waste water, which means there is less need
for treatment. In the end, less treatment means less energy, which
equals more green points.

Opportunity: Greenhouse Gas Reductions

Some of the most exciting green building possibilities are in the
energy-saving category. It's big because energy prices are higher
than ever, and global warming is a concern. One simple solution
is to purchase a percentage of your business's power through a
green power program. Green power is electricity produced from
wind, geothermal, solar, biomass, and low-impact small hydroelec-
tric resources. It is a subset of renewable energy, which results in
few, if any, greenhouse gas emissions. It is possible to purchase
green power through most electric utilities around the country.
The Environmental Protection Agency has a Green Power Partnership (www.epa.gov/grnpower/) and can be of help in procuring
or understanding it for your organization. The U.S. Green Building Council's minimum criteria for LEED-rated building is that at
least 35 percent of a building's electricity must be from renewable
sources. To that end, and green power programs are an easy way
to get started.

For the more adventuresome, geothermal heating and cooling is another energy- and greenhouse gas-saving winner. It is not
nearly as simple as purchasing green power because it requires running an underground tubing system, so it is not possible to implement if you are leasing space or remodeling on an infill lot in the
city. The concept of geothermal heating and cooling is to use the
relatively constant ground temperature (45°–75°F) to either heat

or cool water running through an underground tube. A few feet below the earth's surface the ground temperature is warmer than the air above it in the winter and cooler in the summer. The geothermal heat pump takes advantage of this mild temperature range and is far more efficient than traditional HVAC and hot water heaters. According to the Environmental Protection Agency, geothermal heating and cooling can reduce energy consumption and corresponding emissions 44–72 percent, depending on the type of equipment it is replacing. The systems can cost several times as much as an air-source system, but the payback period is five to ten years. This will be even less as heating and cooling costs rise.

Another green building idea is to harness the sun. Solar panel technology has been around for many years yet is just beginning to catch on in business applications in this country. Some local governments are even giving incentives to businesses to install solar systems, because solar provides a renewable and nonpolluting source of electricity that can generate power during peak electricity consumption periods. In late 2007, the officials of Rockefeller Plaza in New York City announced that they had installed 363 solar panels on top of the building, making it the largest privately owned solar energy generation station in Manhattan.

It's still difficult to justify a full-blown solar panel system to get a business completely off the grid, but going solar can make sense for clean supplemental energy whether your business is small or large. An engineer or contractor can determine payback periods and savings. These will depend on many variables, such as amount of sunlight the location receives, electricity costs in the area, number of panels, ease or difficulty of installation, and the type of system to be installed. As the price of electricity has increased, so have advances in solar technology and solar awareness, which will ultimately bring the price down. It is also probable that government agencies will start to provide financial incentives to install solar systems as electricity use and costs continues to escalate.

Getting Away from Heat Island

In addition to providing solar energy, the sun's heat can produce heat islands. These are not exotic vacation getaways. Less vegetation and more hard, dark, man-made surfaces cause cities to be several degrees hotter than the countryside. Over 90 percent of the roofs in the United States are dark in color, and under a hot summer sun the surface temperature can reach nearly 200°F. Some of that heat transfers to the buildings' interiors. During the summer, power needed from coal-fired power plants to fuel air conditioners to counteract this heat island effect causes more air pollution, greenhouse gases, and smog.

Businesses can limit the heat island effect by minimizing dark surfaces on their roofs. One effective and inexpensive way to do this is to use reflective roof coatings or cool roof technologies. This is a particularly wise strategy if your business is located in the southern half of the United States. Many capable contractors do this kind of work, and savings can be 20–70 percent off your annual cooling bill. Some cities, like Chicago, are now mandating that a certain amount of solar reflectance be used on roofs of new commercial buildings. California has a Cool Savings Program that provides rebates to building owners for installing cool roofing materials.

Lighting for your business should be cool and stylish. There are many new lighting technologies available when building new or significantly remodeling. Some are mentioned in Chapter 4. The most compelling idea is to design space that uses natural daylight. This can be done using clear or opaque glass or plastic panels in walls, rather than solid sheetrock. If the space is designed well, less electricity will be used to light it during daylight hours. Consider installing light sensors for overhead lights to make sure the lights are turned on only if there isn't enough brightness from the outdoors. A properly sized and designed system of skylights, windows, and sensors can allow for the electric lights to be turned off as much as 70 percent of the year, saving a good chunk of change, energy, and power plant emissions.

Natural lighting is a universal human need. Our moods and our happiness are connected to getting enough sunlight. Our alertness and energy levels are affected by a lack of daylight. Anyone suffering from seasonal affective disorder knows this fact all too well. Working in the daylight has been found to help improve morale, increase sales, and even decrease absenteeism. A study, *Daylight and Retail Sales,* conducted by the California Energy Commission discovered that stores with skylights had a 40 percent higher sales volume compared to those without skylights. Also, there was an increase in the number of transactions per month, and employees expressed higher satisfaction with their work environment.

Other exciting new lighting technologies are being developed and tested and seem promising for cutting our electric use in buildings even further. One system pipes sunlight into a building through optical fibers, which feed the light into an acrylic rod and diffuses full spectrum sunlight into a room. This kind of lighting is virtually electricity-free and can be combined with fluorescent tubes for night or cloudy days. Soon this new technology will be available on a wide scale and at a competitive price.

Light-emitting diode (LED) technology is also a good possibility for future lighting alternatives in buildings. Even though a single LED is tiny, a special lens can diffuse the light, or many LEDs grouped together can be placed in the same fixture, creating the same effect as traditional lighting. LEDs are much more earth friendly than ordinary light bulbs because they have a long life; they burn cool, requiring only a small amount of electricity; and they are nontoxic (unlike fluorescent bulbs that contain toxic mercury). Other cost-effective lighting technologies are being developed and tested. It is only a matter of time before incandescent and even fluorescent bulbs will be obsolete.

Opportunity: Green Building Products

A very important cornerstone of green building is good indoor air quality, and green building products are the key. We've all heard horror stories of Legionnaires' disease and sick building syndrome, when people have become sick or died due to tainted indoor air. But the more typical scenarios involve employees with recurring headaches at work or frequent asthma attacks. When you begin a remodel or new build process, doing as much as possible to keep your indoor air quality clean will pay off in a healthier and happier staff.

If you take a look around in most business-owned buildings, you will see that nearly everything is made from petroleum. The floors are covered in carpet or tiles that are petroleum based. The walls are covered in wallpaper or paint that is made from petroleum. The ceiling tiles of drop-down ceilings are produced from petroleum. Most office furniture has a high plastic content, which is made from petroleum. Likewise, most office equipment is made from petroleum-based plastic. All products made from petroleum give off volatile organic compounds (VOCs). VOCs are organic chemical compounds that vaporize under normal conditions (such as the chemical smell from a latex or oil-based paint). New buildings have concentrations of VOCs two to ten times higher than older buildings. VOCs are suspected causes of everything from asthma to cancer, so it is in everyone's best interest to limit the amount of petroleum-derived products in any indoor environment.

One way to protect your indoor air quality is to purchase building materials that contain fewer or no VOCs. Finding paints that have no or low VOCs used to be a chore, but now they are as close as your neighborhood paint store. Every major paint brand has a no- or low-VOC option. The paint comes in the same great colors as the traditional paints and will apply as easily but has virtually no odor. Building occupants will not experience headache, nausea, or asthma attacks as a result of a freshly painted room. There are plenty of low-emitting materials if you look for them, such as nontoxic adhesives, solvents, sealants, wood products like particleboard, and carpets.

To improve your building's indoor air quality, use as many natural materials as possible. Forego the synthetic-covered furniture and choose organic cotton, wool, or even leather fabrics. Buy furniture frames made from certified sustainably forested wood made by local craftsman. Have as many hard surface walkways as possible made from natural rubber or concrete. Limit carpeted areas to cubicles and offices for sound deadening only where you need it. Remember that hard surfaces can easily be cleaned, unlike carpet, which holds allergens and dust mites. These are just a few examples of how to keep air in mind when building green.

Certification Programs

The green building industry is maturing. It has developed widely accepted standards administered by trusted entities. This makes it easier for businesspeople to start making proper green building choices. Even if you don't care if your building is certified green, it is a good idea to do some research and look into the various certification programs. Most national and regional certification programs are geared toward building professionals rather than business owners, but they still are a good place to get a sense of the options available. Such programs typically include checklists of environmental attributes used to rate a building, including a point system for indoor air quality, energy performance, and resource use.

The most widely known and accepted rating system for commercial buildings is the Leadership in Energy and Environmental Design (LEED) Green Building Rating System from the U.S. Green Building Council (USGBC). While there are several regional rating systems that have been developed, LEED, so far, is the most widely used nationally accepted rating system. In addition to providing specific project certifications, architects, builders, and designers can get professional accreditation through the LEED program by taking classes and passing a test to ensure that they are knowledgeable about sustainable building basics. The USGBC's website (*www.usgbc.org*) is a good starting point for either thinking through the possibilities for your project or for finding a green builder or architect in your area. The American Institutes of Architects (*www.aia.org*) is another good place to find green building qualified designers and architects.

Green building products can still be a confusing morass. It can be difficult to find out if a manufacturer's earth-friendly claims are true, but there are a few product categories that provide third-party verification. One of the oldest and most well respected certification programs is for wood. The Forest Stewardship Council (FSC) label promises that the wood was grown in a sustainably managed forest, using no clear cutting. The U.S. government's Energy Star program is well-respected and certifies the energy efficiency of various electronics and equipment including appliances, heating and cooling equipment, office equipment, and lighting. Green Seal certifies products for a growing list of green building-related products, including paints, coatings, windows, and doors.

Easy Steps to Green

Following are six helpful tips to get you started with a successful green building project. Anything earth friendly that you can do in the process of building new or remodeling will be positive for the environment. You don't need to spend beyond your means or have a certified green building, but greener is better. The benefits will far outweigh the costs and hassles of doing it in an earth-friendly fashion.

1. Make It Somebody's Job

Remodeling or building from the ground up can be over-whelming for any size organization. Add the green component to the project and eyes may start to roll, heads to swim. Green building is so new that it is still a practice and not yet a full-blown industry. Many professionals, like architects and contractors, are still trying to figure out their own knowledge base and how to offer it to clients. Many green building products are in an experimental state compared to the old tried-and-true methods of traditional construction. A green building project needs oversight from a well-connected insider from the organization. This person needs to lead the charge with the management team, make decisions, and be capable of building consensus. Don't overlook that she or he also needs to be interested in learning everything possible about green building as it relates to your business and your building. This person will ultimately be responsible for guiding the project and deciding which green components will be included and those that won't. There are ample resources on the web and in print to help the chosen one become a quick study.

2. Find Local Professionals

Do an Internet search for green buildings built in your area. Contact the building owner or management firm to find out whom they used for design and construction general contracting. Most of the pioneer green building owners who are touting green buildings are more than happy to talk to other organizations about their experience. Directly ask them if they were happy with their choice of professional and if they would use that company or contractor again. If you are the first to build or remodel green in a town or city, go to the websites of the U.S. Green Building Council and the American Institute of Architects to find a green building professional nearby. If that fails, and it is price prohibitive to bring in an out-of-town architect, you can do what I did over a decade ago and general contract the project in-house. My colleagues and I learned as much as we could about green building, put one of our employees in charge of the project, and taught our vendors and subcontractors about green building.

3. Have Several Brainstorming Meetings

Some architects call planning or brainstorming meetings design charrettes (pronounced *shuh-ret*). They can be very useful as an organization sorts through its green building needs and wants. Design charrettes involve stakeholders of the green building project—typically representatives from the various parts of the organization that will occupy the building. The goal of the charrette is to educate the stakeholders about the various green options as you begin to design the project and get their ideas of what they want. It is also meant to get agreement from key individuals in the business at the outset of the project. A design charrette can be facilitated by an architect, designer, or by someone skilled in facilitation and construction from within the organization.

4. Apply the Three Rs

Once you have your green building wish list from the design charrettes, sort and prioritize the list of possibilities. Energy efficiency improvements are fairly glaring these days—if it saves money and the payback period is reasonable, go for it. If you are working with an architect or designer, she should be able to give you approximate costs and payback periods for each component. Once a budget is determined, use the three Rs of recycling—reduce, reuse, and recycle—to guide you through some of the less obvious priorities. When remodeling a space, instead of changing the concrete flooring that is in good shape choose to stain it. That's an example of reducing materials by not replacing something unless necessary. Purchase previously used stone countertops for use in the new reception area. This is as an example of the reuse of materials to update an old look. And use deconstruction techniques, rather than tearing down the building and carting it away in a dumpster. That's an example of recycling.

5. Look for Pots of Green Money

Sometimes a green building will cost more than a traditional building. You can justify the extra expense only by acknowledging and recognizing the tradeoffs. Look for life cycle benefits of green. For example, you can add five to seven years of life to carpeted areas by installing a slightly more expensive natural rubber floor for the walking paths through an office rather than installing the typical wall-to-wall carpet. Foot traffic will be mostly confined to the more durable rubber flooring and carpet can still be installed under desks or cubicles for sound deadening purposes.

Be sure to check into federal and local grants, subsidies, and low-interest loans for installing things that government agencies and nonprofits want to promote, like solar power in California. More funding programs are becoming available all the time as agency priorities shift with changing politics. Taxes and fees on things that governments want to discourage are also becoming more common. Make sure your green building plan is structured to maximize incentives on things that should be encouraged and minimize disincentives such as fees or taxes on behaviors that need to be discouraged. A good example of a newer government-imposed fee is outdoor hard surface areas, which are being taxed to account for polluted runoff water entering storm sewers.

Insurance companies are beginning to understand that green buildings eliminate many risks. You can find preferential rates in the form of credits and policy upgrades for buildings that have been certified green. For example, the Fireman's Fund has a program available for U.S. Green Building Council LEED-certified buildings.

Some mortgage industry experts are predicting that by 2012 green mortgages or energy mortgages with preferential rates and terms for green buildings will be widely available. This trend will be driven by nationally accepted green building standards and more widely accepted certification programs along with the need to increase energy and resource efficiency in the United States.

6. Consider Green Building Certification

If you are going to build a new green building, it may make sense to have it certified. Yes, it adds steps to the building process, and it adds costs in the form of third-party oversight professional fees, but it also ultimately may add value to the real estate. This is a good option to consider if the real estate is owned by the organization occupying it. Certification will also make it possible to qualify for some ongoing expense reductions mentioned previously. And the building will stand up better under public and media scrutiny if you decide to publicize your greenness.

Chapter 6

Greening the Outside Space—
Lawns, Plants, Drives, and Roofs

The old environmental adage, "Everybody lives downstream" is especially true for me. I live in Minneapolis on the Mississippi River only a few hundred miles from where the river starts, and it seems that everybody in the middle of the country does live downstream from me. Well, that's not exactly true. Our drinking water comes from the Mississippi River. Before it reaches us, it has already gone through hundreds of miles of farmland, which contribute pesticides, herbicides, and manure to the water that I drink everyday. Fortunately it has been cleaned up in a state-of the-art water treatment facility just north of Minneapolis.

The water runs through Minneapolis on its way to St. Paul, collecting rainwater and snow melt runoff from every piece of property in the greater metropolitan area. This runoff flows into the nearest city street culvert. From the culvert the runoff water makes its way into the nearest body of water—creek, pond, or lake—and then into the Mississippi River. Our Minnesota water then moves south through the country ultimately dumping into the ocean near New Orleans, used and reused by many millions of people and farms along the way. Where the river runs into the Gulf of Mexico, there is an enormous dead zone—the size of New Jersey—where no marine life exists. That's because of all the pollutants the Mississippi collects on its journey through the continent.

The pollution that we accidentally add to the water via our storm sewers as it runs through Minneapolis affects everyone downstream. These seemingly small acts of pollution—fertilizer that is applied to lawns, oil and transmission fluid that drips out of a car or truck while it's parked in the neighborhood strip mall, or salt from an icy winter road—add up when one considers the millions of people, homes, businesses, and roads that contribute to the problem. Now factor in the runoff from farms and the effluent from factories located along water resources and you have a recipe for disaster. The pollution is so great, in fact, that it overwhelms our rivers' natural abilities to clean and heal themselves. The end result is lifeless, tasteless, and potentially dangerous water.

We live in a time when rivers and lakes no longer burn from massive amounts of pollution like they did in the 1970s, but we may have been lulled into a false sense of security about water pollution. While many of the pollution sources (for example, effluent-belching pipes from power plants and industry) are regulated and relatively clean, unregulated nonpoint source toxic runoff still comes from yards, parking lots, farms, and roads.

We haven't even talked about drought-induced water shortages, structures built where nature did not intend (shorelines, wetland, and floodplains), and the growing cost of useable water. It can be overwhelming. But do not despair. There is still much a business can do to be part of the solution. This chapter will give you real-world answers for protecting our water resources from runoff, reducing water costs, and decreasing landscape maintenance costs while beautifying the exterior of your workplace.

All businesses and organizations own or lease space in a building. Even a self-employed person working from home is located in a structure. We all have the ability to influence in a large or small way the outdoor space around our location.

Opportunity: Storm Water Management

You don't need to live on the Mississippi River to be concerned about water. No matter where you are in the world, you are in a watershed—everyone lives downstream from someone else. Fresh water constantly moves around the planet in the form of rain and snow, falls to the ground, and either is absorbed into the soil, adding to the groundwater, or runs off the land, adding to surface water of lakes, rivers, and streams. No matter where we are, we affect our watershed and the water quality by what we do on land. Watershed health, and with it our drinking water quality, depend on how we manage precipitation as it lands on our property and leaves it. This is called storm water management. The main goal of storm water management is to have water absorb into the soil where it can be cleaned naturally by layers of rock, sand, and organisms rather than run off the land, carrying pollution with it.

A simple way to reduce runoff at your property is to build a rain garden. A rain garden is a strategically located swale or depression in the ground that will collect rainwater or melting snow from roofs, gutter systems, and parking lots. Plant the swale with native, water-slurping plants that absorb the runoff, keeping it on the property and ultimately returning it to the ground water. This keeps polluted water from running into rivers and streams. It also allows a natural cleansing of water prior to its return to the water system. You can build rain gardens anywhere.

A bioretention area is a slightly more complicated and intensely engineered rain garden. Storm water again goes into a shallow ditch or swale, but it filters down through the ground and collects in a drainpipe. Then, the clean water is discharged elsewhere.

If you are constructing, reconstructing, or restriping a parking lot, keep green in mind. One of the most effortless storm water management innovations is known as green parking. Green parking lots use a combination of design techniques to limit storm water runoff. If you make the length and width of each individual parking stall smaller, more spaces can fit into the lot. Reducing the size of anything in our super-sized culture may seem challenging, but it will allow you to have more parking on less land, which has the added benefit of reducing hard surfaces where water easily runs off.

Provide compact car or hybrid car parking spaces close to the door, near handicapped spaces, to encourage employees and patrons to drive smaller, more fuel-efficient vehicles. This is low cost and stimulates environmentally responsible behavior. In that same line of reasoning, put larger spaces for SUVs and trucks near the back of the lot. If you can, share a parking lot with another business. This can work well if one has parking needs during the day—for instance, an office—and the other has parking needs at night—a restaurant or bar. This eliminates the need for two separate lots and cuts down on hard surface.

One caution before you forge ahead with the new parking space plan. Some of these space-sizing and location techniques may require a variance from city codes, because government regulations haven't kept pace with environmental innovation. Even though this kind of parking design should be encouraged by governmental agencies, they have yet to catch up with marketplace needs.

One more storm water management technique is to install pavers that allow water to soak into the ground, rather than installing an impervious surface like concrete or asphalt. Alternative pavers are made with either permeable and semipermeable materials. One paver commonly used is cement-paving blocks with gravel or grass planted in spaces inside or around the blocks. Other permeable materials include:

> Cobbles

> Bricks

> Turf blocks

> Natural stone

> Wood mulch

> Gravel

Even though this kind of parking surface soaks up water effectively, there are limitations. Alternative pavers do best in warmer climates and are not as effective in cold climates where snow plowing and de-icing are needed. In those regions of the country, it may be best to limit alternative pavers to overflow and low-traffic parking lots.

Opportunity: Green Space

Green vegetation absorbs water and returns it to the ground, rather than allowing it to run off. It also helps reduce greenhouse gases. Vegetation acts as a sponge to absorb carbon dioxide (a greenhouse gas), helping to slow down or at least not add to global warming. Green space is good.

Green space is also beneficial, because it gives us a psychological boost. In addition to the environmental benefits, green spaces just plain make you feel good. Going out for a walk to get some air in a natural setting when you feel overwhelmed or stressed out from work helps to calm you down and be more focused. You don't get quite the same good feelings walking on the street where there is traffic, noise, and lots of activity. This is not some granola girl philosophy. Surrounding ourselves with nature is a normal human need. There is a growing body of psychological research that confirms contact with nature increases mental health. Richard Louv's book, *Last Child in the Woods: Saving our Children from Nature Deficit Disorder,* discusses the research that indicates exposure to the natural world is essential for the physical and emotional health of both children and adults. Steven and Rachel Kaplan, of the University of Michigan, and Terry Hartig, of Uppsala University, have shown that time in nature (even in small amounts) leads to faster renewed attention and restored mental clarity after taxing mental tasks. These health benefits are often overlooked, but will encourage productivity from employees, which equals good business. Another less-talked-about benefit is that pocket parks and grassy areas with trees help to reduce the heat island effect discussed in Chapter 5.

But green space need not be green in color. The problem with most green space is that it is turf, in other words grass-centric. Turf needs to be mowed on a weekly basis and can cause more harm to the environment than good. Lawn mowers are typically gasoline powered and run by two-cycle engines, which are heavy air polluters because they do not have emission controls as vehicles do. One hour of mowing with a gasoline-powered mower is equivalent to the emissions from driving 350 miles in a car, which adds to smog and air quality problems in cities. Maybe even more sickening is that 17 million gallons of gas is spilled annually from refueling lawn and garden equipment.

By 2011, a federal mandate will require that most new mowers sold in the United States must filter out an additional thirty-five pollutants using similar technology to auto exhaust systems. Many of the major brands for both home and commercial lawn mowers sell a model with a four-stroke or cycle engine that burns cleaner because the oil is separate from the fuel. If your lawn company or maintenance staff is using old equipment with a two-stroke engine that burns a polluting oil–gas mixture, the new law will not help you. Insist that maintenance crews use four-cycle engine mowers for now, and by 2011 require in your lawn maintenance contract that they use the new, more efficient equipment. Of course, electric or battery-powered mowers for smaller plots of grass are another less-polluting and quieter alternative.

We love green grass in this country, but it isn't the most earth-friendly ground cover. "No mow" green space is better. Grass doesn't grow naturally in most parts of the country, so it takes a tremendous amount of water, fertilizer, and weed control to achieve the look that most people want. If you are building new construction or preparing to relandscape, severely limiting grass is by far the greenest option. As an alternative to grass, design and landscape with plants native to the area. Native plants are resistant to disease and drought, add visual interest, and reduce mowing.

> *Prairie:* Drought-resistant tall grasses and wild flowers.

> *Desert:* Cactus and other succulents that store water in their leaves and stems

> *Woodlands:* Ferns, black cohosh, trillium, and other plants native to the cooler, more wooded Northwest

Native plants at one time grew naturally and were able to survive without any artificial inputs. They had adapted to their climate and soil conditions, flourishing with only rainwater and needing no fertilizer or pest control. For this reason they're the perfect low-maintenance and low-cost green space vegetation.

Some of the most upscale commercial developments and corporate campuses are sporting native landscaping, but it is also starting to catch on with smaller facilities and office buildings. There are obviously some up-front costs to remove the grass and replant with natives, nurturing the young plants for several seasons, but the benefits are well worth it. Watering will be nearly eliminated. And once the plants are healthy and mature, weeds and pests will be crowded out so there is no need for herbicides or pest control. Mowing, with its noise, air pollution, and cost, will be only a memory. Native plants will also attract wildlife like birds and butterflies to your property, giving workers a better connection to the natural world and a better attitude.

Switching to organics for whatever plant food you use on your commercial property is another way to be greener outside. For years, businesses have used synthetic or petroleum-based fertilizers and herbicides on their grounds. In the long run, that results in depleted soil and polluted runoff. Organics for lawns or gardens encourage healthy soil full of microorganisms. If the lawn has been on toxic chemicals for years, it will take a couple of growing seasons on organics to look full and lush again. To get started, skip the chemical lawn treatments and begin organic lawn treatments made from once-living things, such as fish emulsion made from partially decomposed, pulverized fish. Weeds can be stopped in the lawn with an all-natural pre-emergent made from corn gluten. If you have plants in gardens or containers, start over by amending the soil to get the nutrients back in to the upper surface. Combine a mixture of organic soil, organic peat moss, and organic compost or manure for a rich planting medium that will hold water and have the proper microorganisms for optimal plant health. If the grounds are large enough, you can even start a compost pile of leaves and chipped tree debris to add to your containers or gardens.

Organic gardening treats plants, trees, and grass as a part of a whole system and results in lush soil, happy wildlife, beneficial insects, and healthy people. Once the soil is amended, plant organic seeds or plants. Look for the "certified organic" seal on the packet. Certified organic starter plants can be hard to find, but growers who use organic practices are becoming more common. Talk to your local nursery or landscaper and find out if synthetic chemical pesticides and fertilizers were used to raise the plants. Once the plants are established, be sure to use organic fertilizers and herbicides—fertilizers made from once-living things such as fish or animal blood are all natural. Nonsynthetic chemical herbicides made from vinegar and citric acids are becoming more widely available as well.

For green extra credit, go to the next level of greenness and plant edible, organically grown herbs and berries. Imagine stepping outside of your office building to nibble on a raspberry from a bush in the green space or grab some fresh basil from the herb garden for your lunch sandwich.

Taking special care of the living things on the outside of your building or facility will say something positive to the people who work on the inside. A visible cue like landscaping sends the message of caring that is good for employee morale. They realize that you are taking care of the bigger picture, the environment, and will take care of them too. Everyone who walks into your building will—even if only subconsciously—get the good, green message.

Opportunity: Water Savings

Keeping our water resources clean is essential. Cutting down on water use outside of our buildings is another idea whose time has come. The price of water is rising all over the country, in some cases by as much as 100 percent, as many cities and towns try to repair or replace aging water infrastructure. In high population growth areas like the Southwest where water is scarce and expensive to deliver, prices have risen even faster. Add to this the many drought-stricken areas of the country and you can see that water cost and availability are growing concerns for businesses.

As water costs rise, xeriscaping has become more popular in the Southwest and Southeast where rain is never dependable. The term *xeriscaping* combines *xeros*, the Greek word for dry, with *landscaping* to express the concept of attractive landscapes based on plants that use little water. Xeriscaping plants are chosen for their lack of thirst. A proper mix can result in much less water use—less than half than that used to maintain turf.

Sometimes xeriscaping is confused with *zeroscaping*. They are not the same, even though they both use less water than the old traditional wall-to-wall green grass approach. Zeroscaping uses rock and hard surfaces to create a hard, cold, and often not-very-interesting design. On the other hand, xeriscaping can be lush, embracing a wide variety of plants and some mulch to create an oasis on the driest property. Use organic mulches made from bark and wood grindings. Be careful not to put plastic under mulch or rocks, because it will encourage shallow root systems by preventing the soil from breathing. To promote lush plants in dry regions, it is essential they have a deep root system.

The benefits of xeriscaping are much the same as planting natives. First, it saves time and money—and in business, time is money. Second, typical turf lawns are thirsty. Xeriscaping eliminates or de-emphasizes grasses like bluegrass that need a lot of water. Your costs will be reduced in the form of lower water bills and less maintenance expense. The financial benefits are obvious when there is less or no mowing, weeding, and fertilizing.

Whether you are in a northern or a southern climate, properly planning an irrigation system will also save water. Irrigate turf areas on separate zones from natives or xeriscape plants, which will need little to no water. Spray lawns by sprinklers, but use low-volume drip emitters to water ground cover, trees, shrubs, and flowers. Be sure to run your irrigation systems before or after the heat of the day, so that the water doesn't evaporate into the air rather than getting to the plant roots. For years low-tech rain gauges have been available to stop irrigation systems from turning on if there has been a recent storm. Now it is possible to find irrigation controllers that are linked to a GPS satellite so that the system waters based on weather conditions and not just time or evaporating water levels in a rain gauge.

Capturing graywater for irrigation is a newer technology that is also becoming more popular. Graywater is water that has been used for showers, hand-washing, and laundry. It is not to be confused with blackwater, which comes from toilets and needs to go into the sewer system. When constructing or remodeling your facility, you can separate graywater and blackwater into two systems by running different lines. A tank collects the graywater instead of running it into the sewer or septic system. You'll also need a filter and special emitters to set up a graywater irrigation system.

Before you decide on installing a graywater system, there are a couple of considerations to research. Installing such a system can be costly, so be sure to analyze the payback period based on the cost of water and the amount of vegetation on the property. There may also be extra requirements by your local or state health department, special permits, or licensing. Check with your local agencies. If you can install a graywater system at a reasonable cost, it is an excellent way to save water and lower ongoing operating costs.

Opportunity: Green Roof

Even if the building you work in has no outdoor space for grass or trees, it still has a roof. Green roofs are a great opportunity to expand your green building features.

For some the mere mention of a green or a vegetative roof brings up giggles and images of Heidi in the Alps, Hobbit homes in Middle Earth, or, stranger yet, Teletubbies. Others worry that green roofs will need lots of maintenance (how the heck do you get a lawn mower up there?). Another concern is that a green roof will add a tremendous amount of weight to a roof. Despite these fears and misconceptions, green roofs are quickly becoming all the rage in our largest cities.

Rooftop gardens with trees and grass, which you might see on buildings around Central Park in New York, are one type of green roof. This type of green roof does add weight with its knee-deep soil used to grow plants. But more recently, innovation has spawned a new technology for growing living things on roofs. You can spread a thin layer of lightweight growing medium seeded with plants able to thrive in rooftop climates that are hot, dry, very windy, and have an excess of sunshine. The end result is more like a prairie with grasses and wildflowers, different from a park with grass, shrubs, and trees. The weight of this type of green roof is comparable to a gravel ballast roof. It costs about twice as much as a regular roof, but it will help the roof last two to three times as long because the plants protect the roof from radiation and temperature extremes.

Heidi's goat-herding family in the Alps was on to something. The life-extending quality of a green roof is only one of its many benefits. Green roofs are also energy efficient with a quantifiable heating and cooling savings. The added insulation of the plants and growing medium on the roof keep the building cooler in the summer and warmer in the winter, which translates into less energy use and lower utility bills. Because rainwater and snow that lands on the roof is absorbed by the plants and growing medium, a green roof will help keep your water supply clean by not letting melted snow or rainwater leave the roof. Also plants, roots, and dirt are great natural filters and can clean heavy metals from polluted air and minimize any excess toxin-laden water that might otherwise drain into storm sewers. Having green space on top of buildings, rather than a dark, hard surface, also helps reduce the heat island effect, since it absorbs heat and sunlight. Green roofs can also help slow global warming since the green vegetation possesses the ability to absorb greenhouse gases.

This isn't just some wild idea. Green roofs have been popular in Europe for decades. Greening Gotham is a New York City green roof project whose goal is to cool down the metropolis and use less energy. Mayors in cities like Atlanta, Chicago, and Toronto have decided to make cooling and greening their rooflines a priority. In 2008 the New York state legislature passed a bill that gives building owners who install a green roof on at least 50 percent of their available rooftop a one-year property tax credit of up to $100,000. The credit equals approximately 25 percent of the typical cost of installing a green roof.

It may sound like a big undertaking to install a green roof, but the technology and expertise have evolved quickly in the past several years. A good time to embark on a green roof project is when you are either constructing a new building or replacing the roof on an existing one. First, find a designer or engineer capable of analyzing the current structure's capacity to carry the weight of a green roof. The designer should also be able to suggest materials and an experienced contractor. It is best to work with someone with vegetative roof experience both in the design and construction phases. Look for a landscape architect, engineer, architect, or designer. Additionally, you can check with your local government offices to see if they encourage green roofs and if they have a list of contractors. You can also find out if there are any rebate or tax credit programs to help you with the project, or if there are any local codes or ordinances to prevent you from vegetating your roof. The local chapter of the U.S. Green Building Council (*www.usgbc.org*) or the American Institute of Architects (*www.aia.org*) are other good resources.

Easy Steps to Green

Following are five helpful tips to get you started with successful earth-friendly outdoor projects. It is easy to overlook your outdoor space, because it is away from any meaningful part of the business. But from a green standpoint, the outside space is just as important as the inside space and perhaps has a greater impact on the environment. It is time that you look at an entire property—building, parking, and grounds—as a living, breathing ecosystem that fits within the larger local ecosystem on the planet. Anything that you do—good or bad—in your microecosystem affects everything else in the larger environment.

1. Identify Trigger Points to Begin Greening Outside

Perhaps it's time to build a new facility, expand the existing one, or repave the parking lot. Any change in the physical exterior structure should signal an opportunity for you to consider implementing something new and green. If it is time to repave the parking lot, make sure that someone is asking the green questions: Can we add some rain gardens? Can we make our parking spaces smaller to get more cars in the lot in order to include rain gardens? When it is time to reroof or build a new facility, call a green roof designer and ask about the feasibility of a vegetative roof. If you are leasing the facility, your leverage point is when you are signing a lease or renewing a lease. Use that leverage to request the landlord do something green to the exterior. Ask about switching to organics, planting natives, or xeriscaping. Don't let the opportunity for greening pass you by—use it!

2. Make Greening a Priority During Contract Negotiations

If you own or are managing the property, use contract time with a landscape company to demand less-polluting techniques. Use the negotiations with the contractor as a teachable moment. Tell the contractor that you want to start using organics on the lawn, and find out how he can accommodate the request. Ask about what kind of lawn equipment he is using, and insist on less-polluting equipment, like four-cycle mowers. If the contractor agrees to these kinds of requests, memorialize them into the contract with penalties for noncompliance. If he doesn't agree, find a contractor who will. You may be the first in your area to ask for these kinds of green changes, but you won't be the last.

3. Find Local Experts

Finding local expertise is the fastest way to get the best green results. Take advantage of the hard-earned knowledge from people who have greened their own or a client's landscaping or roof. It will help keep you from getting lost in the weeds on the project. Talk to fellow business associates who are implementing green, and find out whom they have used. Get creative. If you can't find someone who does native landscaping or xeriscaping for commercial buildings, check in the residential sector. If you are the first in your area to tackle these innovations, find the closest city with a U.S. Green

Building Council chapter or talk to your state's pollution control office to find experienced consultants and contractors.

4. Check Local Ordinances and Codes

Whether you are a large company with multiple sites around the country or a smaller organization in a single location, find a way to keep tabs on the laws that might affect your greening plans. In many locations, city ordinances and building codes have not yet caught up with green building practices. For example, there may be a local weed ordinance that will prohibit you from planting natives or xeriscaping. There may also be local requirements for drives and parking lots that determine the number of parking spaces or the kind of surface. It is important to know these requirements before you get too far into the planning stages of a permeable paver drive or smaller parking stalls. If you run into a municipal roadblock, try to get a variance for your project. You just may be the first to get this issue on the city's radar screen.

5. Look for Rebates and Credits

Some cities and states are trying to encourage various green building innovations by giving rebates or credits. For example, Albuquerque, New Mexico, offers a water bill credit to encourage less water use through xeriscaping. The amount of the rebate is based on the number of square feet that is landscaped with plants that use less irrigation water. Portland, Oregon, also has programs to encourage the installations of green roofs. These incentives change as the perception of environmental problems rise in priority. Not only do priorities change, but political interests and the will of a community change as well. So it is best to check with the city, county, and state to find out if there is a current program that will help make your green project a little more feasible.

Chapter 7

Greening the Operation— People, Policies, and Practices

In the early days of my company's greening, we had a good-natured rivalry with other socially responsible businesses. We competed on the basis of who could give their employees the most ethical incentives to inspire environmentalism and good old-fashioned trust. We tried practices like four-day workweeks, full-time telecommuting, and allowing employees to take as much vacation time as they wanted. We experimented with socially responsible policies, because treating people in the same way that we wanted to be treated was a big part of our corporate culture. It worked. We have consistently attracted and kept the best people in the business. We have also stayed true to the golden rule, which is the foundation of our corporate culture and keeps it strong. Somewhere along the way we found that greening the people, policies, and practices helped employees maintain work-life balance.

The term *operation* is used in this chapter to differentiate it from both the physical space in which a business is conducted and the product the business produces, whether it's a widget or a service. Operation is a catchall for everything else in a business. It boils down to people, policies, and practices. It is the nitty-gritty of business. Without a good operational foundation, the wheels come off. It is the area of business where greening is the least defined and has the most promise for creativity and big impacts. The only limit for greening the operation is the imagination of the people involved. The ideas in this chapter have all been successfully implemented in organizations. This chapter is meant to give you a taste of what is possible in order to get your creative juices flowing. I hope that someday soon you can best your competitors with innovative programs for the sake of all on the planet.

The benefits of greening an operation usually translate into saved money each time you save energy, whether it's carbon-based energy from a delivery vehicle or human energy from an office worker. But greening an operation is so much more beneficial than just saving a little money here or there. In fact, some green practices will cost money rather than save it (implementing an organic food program, reimbursing employees for switching to compact fluorescents light bulbs at home, and so on). Even so, the benefits of some of these initiatives still far outweigh the costs. These are invaluable green strategies you can implement to ensure you attract and keep good employees. In any business, a stable, dedicated, and passionate staff is priceless.

Speaking of values, how important is it that you attract talent who shares your company's values—or personal values, for that matter? A growing segment of the work force is looking first and foremost for meaningful work. They come from all walks of life. They are just out of college, middle-aged career changers, or senior citizens who are looking to give their time, talent, and energy to a company they can believe in. They are desperate to work for an employer who cares about them and, maybe even more critically, cares about the broader community and planet. They are committed and passionate workers. This is the real coup with going green—attracting the best and brightest. Meaningful work is the feel-good stuff that we all, deep down, want and need in our lives.

Opportunity: Paperless

Perhaps the dream of the paperless office was overrated in the 1990s when it was first touted as a real possibility. Computers, digital storage, and the Internet seemed to make it more feasible, but, strangely, paper use actually went up, not down, in the years since. This is all the more reason to make using less paper a big part of a greening any business. The benefits to the bottom line and the planet are substantial when you take into account the true costs of moving, storing, accessing, and sourcing paper compared to digitized information.

Many businesses fail to automate today, even though the technology is available, because they believe it will be hugely expensive.

Don't fall into this trap. Using less paper can save any organization big bucks, no matter what its size. Keep an open mind and take a fresh look at automation, which allows us to do more with less.

In 1998, I decided to make my property management firm a paperless operation. I wanted my company to be the first in the industry to be paperless. I had attended a lecture by a lawyer in a Chicago law firm who was successful in making his organization paperless. Certainly, I thought, if lawyers could do it, with all their briefs, case transcripts, and court filings, a property management firm could do it. My company used a tremendous amount of paper in those days. We managed buildings, but our service provided owners of property and occupants of property a real person to talk to. The glue that held those relationship together was a continuous stream of paper—monthly financial statements, management reports, work orders, complaints from occupants, bids for improvements, and other things. The paper flowed constantly between the management firm, the owners of the property, the building occupants, and property vendors.

It took longer than we anticipated to become paperless, but in the end we found it was not only possible, it was lucrative. We reduced our labor costs for paper handling, slashed mailing costs, and even saved on storage and office space because we were able to shrink the size of our office. Amid all these benefits, the best thing was that we were able to let about half of our staff work from home. This reduced our office size, saved gas and emissions by not having employees commute, and has made our staff happier. Okay, we are not exactly at zero paper consumption, but we are moving in that direction. As with most things green, it is a journey not a destination.

When we started going paperless, we found that the average cost to send one piece of letter-size mail through the U.S. Postal Service is $8.07. Paper and postage account for only 5 percent of that total; the other 95 percent of the cost is the human labor involved in moving the paper around. Think of the amount of human capital that is expended each time you look for a file, touch a report, or send a physical piece of paper. How many minutes does it take to walk to a file cabinet to find the paper information in a file cabinet, lift it out, copy it, fold it, find an envelope, stuff it in the envelope, put postage on it, and get it to a mail box? The paper envelope must then be picked up by a postal worker in a truck and handled many more times by people and machinery before it reaches its destination. It is then sorted by the destination office, brought to the addressee's desk, and only then is it opened—three days or more after the information was pulled from the original file. A tremendous amount of energy is expended to get the information from point A to point B.

Once we understood this, our goal became to cut down on human energy expended to move the information. We decided we needed to automate three functions that were the most paper and people intensive:

> Building occupant service calls, e.g. what day is the garbage collected or can a satellite dish be installed

> Getting property information to occupants quickly e.g. snow plowing schedules or repair information

> Eliminating paper files of information on each resident

We began by looking at how other industries were automating, reducing phone calls and saving paper. For example, airlines provide a self-service option on their websites allowing you to be your own travel agent and doing away with a paper ticket that is mailed to the traveler. We used this as a model for how we could request and track work orders via the Internet. Another operation from which we took a cue was the relatively new online-banking industry. Many banks allow you to check your balance, review your transaction history, and pay your bills online. We translated this idea for our industry, providing clients with online account statements in real time and property owners with financial reports, delinquency tracking, and bank statements. No longer did we have to mail physical copies of reports.

We also used an online retail store to provide self-service documents to real estate agents and mortgage lenders. We made it possible for them to access all of the information they need via the Internet in order to consummate their transaction. They could request whatever document they needed, then pay for it online with a credit card. We also built a smart e-mail engine so that we could e-mail property notices and announcements to occupants of a building. This gave building managers the ability to send notices from anywhere they had access to a computer. This function really showed us how the paperless system saved big money in labor.

The third building block on this paperless mission was content management—getting all information about a property available to all parties who needed that information whenever they needed it. We built a document management system with various levels of security so that only those authorized could get to the information they needed. This online function has become the repository of all information for each property and each occupant. All information is in one place with easy access anytime, not just when the office is open. Again, no file cabinets or lost or bad information—the paperless property history is forever accessible, backed up, and safe.

The benefits of going paperless have been far more than a reduced bill for paper. No longer depending on paper has given my firm the ability to decentralize our offices and hire workers from anywhere, because they can telecommute. They are able to connect to the information from remote locations. It has also made clients more satisfied, because they can access their own information anytime of the day or night. Out of a dozen paper filing cabinets, only one remains. Currently, we are working on digitizing the last of the paper in those files. Soon we'll be sans filing cabinets.

We have also dramatically downsized our office, because it's no longer used to house file cabinets or employees who are telecommuting from home. The upshot is that we've saved a tremendous amount of resources and costs in staff time, office space, gasoline for commuting, and, of course, paper. Using less paper by automating allowed us to do more with less.

There was another unexpected benefit as well. We were able to repackage our concept into a separate company that sold the software that we had developed, allowing us to share our technology with other management companies around the country. The crazy idea of going paperless turned into a profitable venture that helps other businesses use fewer resources too. As you experiment with green innovation, whether in the area of operations or products, it is possible you'll invent something worthy of being shared. It is entirely possible you'll invent something noteworthy enough that you'll make more money on it than on your core business.

Another big area of paper use is printing and distributing company promotional materials such as brochures, newsletters, and employee information. The printing industry uses lots of toxic materials such as inks, solvents, and press washes. When you bid out a project, choose printers who have switched to less-toxic methods such as biobased cleaning solvents and vegetable- or soy-based inks that won't harm press workers or result in hazardous waste and air emissions. You can also work with a smaller digital printing firm and avoid a large printing press operation. Such firms can produce a print job quickly, so that you can order just what you need, avoiding purchasing in excess.

You can produce and distribute newsletters electronically rather than on paper, saving paper cost and postage. Rethink how your organization touches its customers. Some customers may still want paper, but many would rather have the information electronically.

Send out a survey to a group of your customers to get an idea what kind of contact they really want from you. As for core marketing materials, consider using a brochure for general information, but use your public website for more detailed information. This will keep your company promotional brochure smaller, using less paper and fewer resources. Set up a website for internal company communications to post your company handbook, insurance information, a bulletin board for employees, 401(k) forms, events, and anything else employees need. Give employees paper forms only when you are required by law to have actual signed documents. Even then, scan the document and store it electronically.

When you are buying paper, purchase only recycled-content paper for copiers or printing jobs. If you see the phrase "postconsumer content" on a label, it means the paper has been recycled from previous consumer use at least once. It is greener than postindustrial or preconsumer content, which means it is a waste product but has not yet experienced a first consumer use. The higher percentage of postconsumer, recycled content, the better. Avoid first-use, wood-pulp fiber or virgin fiber as a paper source. It is also possible to buy FSC-certified paper. Just like FSC-certified lumber mentioned in Chapter 5, this is paper made from trees that have been sustainably harvested, their felling certified by a third party. There is also tree-free paper made from quickly growing agricultural plants such as hemps, kenaf, and grasses that are byproducts of other industries. Tree-free paper is widely used in other parts of the world and can be found in the United States, but it is not yet very common or at a competitive price.

Opportunity: Garbage

Bring up the subject of recycling and most people think of bottles, cans, and newspapers. Many businesses still do not recycle these basics. Employees or the CEO might recycle these things at home but not in the office. Maybe the building management or the rubbish hauler has told them it just isn't possible in their building.

The problem with throwing anything away is that it really doesn't go away—it's just away from our sight in a landfill. In the United States we certainly have enough land to safely and effectively store garbage for centuries. The problem with this is that it wastes resources and energy. It takes less energy to remake something than it does to make the same thing from virgin materials. All of the energy used to suck the oil out of the ground, refine it, turn it into a plastic resin, and then mold it into a bag is wasted when the bag is buried in a landfill, where it won't degrade for a very long time. It's far better to turn the bags into another product.

The greenhouse gas connection to recycling often is overlooked. The EPA estimates that if the recycling rate in the United States increased 5 percent, it would decrease greenhouse gas emissions equal to average annual emissions from the electricity consumed by 4.6 million households. Greenhouse gases are emitted in every stage of making and moving plastic objects. Each time that plastic bag can be reused or recycled, it cuts down on emissions and helps reduce global warming. We have gotten better at recycling over the past twenty years, but we still have a long way to go, and business can do better.

As energy and material extraction costs to produce new products increase, it's become easier to recycle all kinds of materials. If you shopped for a hauler of recycled materials, like cardboard, a year or two ago and had trouble, try again. You may now find lots of buyers or haulers for it. The recycled materials market is like the commodities market: it changes constantly.

Gold in Garbage

Rest assured there is almost always someone interested in what you no longer want—one businessperson's trash is another's treasure. Restaurateur Kim Bartman scavenges hotel teardowns for marble and stone that would otherwise end up in a landfill to be used as bar tops and tables in her eateries. A small company, Wipers Recycling, grinds up old leather wingtip shoes into kits that soak up petroleum from oil spills, saving money on raw materials. Midwest Asphalt chops up old roofing shingles, which are 33 percent petroleum, to make new asphalt for drives and walkways saving money and virgin oil. Andersen Windows fuels their boiler system with sawdust from their own plant floors where wood window pieces are sawn.

A good way to start thinking about recycling in a new way is to look around your office or plant to see if waste material is regularly piling up and being carted away. Then start looking for a use for it in your operation. If you can't use it, check into other related or unrelated businesses that might have a use for it. Some state agencies (in Vermont, Minnesota, Massachusetts, and Pennsylvania) are running business material exchange programs to reduce the amount of reuseable materials ending up in landfills. Think of it as a business eBay for waste materials. There is often a state-sponsored website where businesses can register to buy or sell scrap materials, machinery, outdated inventory, packing peanuts, boxes, and many other things. These types of sites often have an "Items wanted" portion of the website, so you can let other businesses know what you are looking for, no matter how unusual it is.

A relatively simple recycling opportunity is to work directly with your vendors to reduce packaging, so that you don't need to recycle as much. As an example, we had an office supply vendor who would double wrap everything they delivered to us. Our client service person realized this and called them to ask if we could have things delivered in a box containing just the original packaging. The extra wrapping and packaging was meant to ensure that everything would arrive in one piece, and the office supply firm considered it good customer service. But they were quick to agree that we could have our office supplies in a box without extra wrap, since it would save them money. You can make this same request of any vendor who delivers goods to your operation. We have had success with lunch vendors, printing vendors, and many others—just politely ask.

Don't overlook recycling electronics. It should be part of an overall green IT plan. Even though there is a movement to green electronics, most cell phones, computer screens, computers, PDAs, and BlackBerries are still made with toxic chemicals and heavy metals that you should not toss in a landfill. These items need to be recycled. If you are a small organization, national electronic retailers have take-back programs in most locations. Some cities have also started to take electronic equipment in their hazardous waste programs. If you're part of a larger organization, you can contract with recyclers to take used electronics off of your hands. It may also be possible to donate used cell phones to a local shelter or outdated computers to a school. Do some research on reuse opportunities before you call the recycler to haul away old equipment.

There are several easy, no cost ways that you can green through policy and practice within your company.

> Encourage everyone in the organization to think before they throw away.

> Make it easy for everyone in your building to recycle.

> Encourage everyone to make copies using both sides of the paper.

> Make it a company practice not to print e-mails unless absolutely necessary.

> Take away individual printers and have only one printer, centrally located.

You will be amazed how much more will get recycled when you set up clearly marked recycling bins in central areas. And if you reduce the number of printers available, this will make printing an e-mail or document slightly more of a hassle. Since the printer is shared by a group of people, employees will begin to police themselves and notice if others are going against policy by printing e-mails.

Opportunity: Green Employee Benefits

Well okay, not green employees, but earth-friendly benefit packages for employees. Turning a company green can be done more effectively when the employees are on board. One way you can send this message is by giving employees the opportunity to be green both at work and at home. An effective way you can do this is by providing employees the option of investing their retirement plans and 401(k) programs in socially responsible investments (SRI). SRI funds favor companies that pay attention to the environment, their employees, and the communities where they operate. It is a great way to walk the green walk and show that you are committed to the environment now and in the future. It can also be a critical part of a benefits package that can attract employees who have a strong environmental ethic. Unfortunately, retirement programs haven't caught up with the green business culture yet, and many 401(k) programs do not offer any SRI funds as investment options. Find out from your company's retirement program liaison or human resources department if you can make this an investment option. If it isn't possible, consider switching to a 401(k) provider that can offer it.

Developing a successful green culture is a byproduct of hiring those who have values aligned with your company's green values and converting the rest of your work force. Green is primarily a learned skill and value system. We are born to cherish the earth, but our culture often contradicts that innate value. Having employee benefits that reinforce green will attract workers with similar values. It is also a good way to help current employees understand green in the context of money.

Another idea to nudge employees toward green is to provide grants, free products, or other incentives for being green at home. This will help you raise awareness about a more earth-friendly life-style. The hope is that your employees will bring this new green attitude back to work. You might give away up to $300 per year in free compact fluorescent light bulbs. Or you might subsidize and organize energy audits for employees' homes. You get the benefits of a greener employee, and your workers can save money on their energy bills without spending their own money to do so. Another possibility you could consider is to pay cash bonuses to employees for being more resource efficient either inside or outside the business.

Giving employees company time to volunteer is not a new idea. But giving paid time off to volunteer for a green cause is a new twist on that idea. Most cities have many environmental nonprofit organizations with volunteer opportunities that range in mission from cleaning up beaches to planting in public green spaces. Provide a list of those organizations to employees and offer one half-day off a month for volunteering. It's a great way to give them a firsthand understanding of what it is to be green. An employee can match her interest with an environmental nonprofit. Some may choose to help plant native oaks in a savannah or cut buckthorn from a riverbank park, while others may accompany kids to a science museum to learn about preserving water resources. No matter the program, a nudge from your company can help get employees active and engaged with the environment.

An additional, and critical, step to leave a green impression on employees is to include the company's green values in the interview process and the employee handbook. This may seem like a simple step, but it is important and often overlooked. I didn't take this step in the early years in my businesses and we would sometimes backslide from our fledgling green company culture when we added new, uninitiated employees. Once the business culture begins to go green, maintaining it can be difficult. Pay attention to how you hire and train new employees; it can make the difference. Make green an explicit feature of your ad when searching for new employees. Let them know that earth friendliness is part of the culture and the expectation in your company. In the interview process explain what the company is doing to be green and what programs, perks, and expectations exist. Put critical information in the employee handbook, outlining the specifics of green benefits so that your employees take advantage of them.

Opportunity: Common Sense

There are some earth-friendly policies and practices that are painless to do and easy to implement. It's all about green common sense. These are all ideas that can work independently from each other and that you can implement over time. Some may work better for one organization than another depending on culture, number of people, and location, but they all benefit the environment and people in a positive way.

Celebrate the environment at least once a year. There was a time when companies used to make a big public relations deal out of this sort of thing. In most cases that time has passed, but there are still good reasons to have an Earth Day, Arbor Day, or another Green Day of your choice. And I mean celebrate. Throw a party. It reminds everyone in the company that the planet supports us in our business and personal lives and is worthy of being celebrated, honored, and appreciated. Have organic champagne. Bring in a speaker. Give away energy-efficient light bulbs. Get outside.

Encourage ongoing education. Both large and small organizations can bring in lunchtime speakers to educate employees about an environmental topic. The topic can be general or specific to an environmental initiative within your company. Advertising the speaker and making the event a regular happening will get the environment in front of employees on a regular basis. Your own green vendors can make good speakers. Talk to the local pollution control agency or an environmental nonprofit and ask them to come in and speak about ideas related to your business or the home.

If you have a cafeteria, serve sustainably grown, organic, and local foods whenever possible. If you don't have food service in your company, compile a list of healthy and organic food options in the neighborhood for employees to consider for lunchtime. If you have a company coffee machine, provide only organic and shade-grown coffee. In our area we have an organic coffee company that delivers coffee to businesses on a bicycle rather than in a truck to cut down on emissions and fuel. Drinking the coffee or seeing the weekly delivery is a good reminder of living green.

Start a program to enable employees to buy a share in a community-supported agriculture (CSA) program. A CSA is a local farm that sells shares in the growing season to individuals. The farm provides "shareholders" with a bushel basket of whatever is being harvested weekly. The food is often organic and always locally owned and supported by the local community. In the good weather months— or anytime in the South—join a CSA and ask for employees to buy a share for their family. Perhaps you could subsidize the program by paying a certain amount for employees who sign on to the program. It helps employees eat healthy, gives them a connection to the real source of food, and it supports locally grown and organic food producers.

Promote greener business meetings in your organization. Ask employees to put their presentations on PowerPoint, not paper.

Make the presentation available electronically before or after the fact. Be conscious about the food and drink served at meetings and what it is served on. Have available reuseable dishes, glasses, and mugs that can be washed rather than disposable ones that are used once and thrown away.

Green your IT department. There are many new, greener IT advances becoming available. Energy Star came out with new specifications in 2007 for office and imaging equipment, which includes accessories that promise significant energy savings for new electronics. Manufacturers are taking the challenge and producing electronics that use 30–75 percent less electricity than standard equipment. For example, some computer companies are selling computers with smaller disk drives that use fewer materials and require less energy to power. Next time you purchase new equipment, ask about its Energy Star rating, and be sure that whatever you buy is the greenest and leanest in energy consumption.

Give green. Any company, no matter how large or small, can consider giving to environmental organizations. Give cash or in-kind donations, or perhaps there are officers in your organization willing to donate their time and organizational skill as board members—or just volunteers.

Implement a "go green" contest. This is a great way to get employees energized about making green changes. Give a bonus or gift to the employee who has the best recycling record or reuse idea. Keep records for a month or a year, rewarding an entire department of the company for reducing paper use or keeping energy costs down by turning off power strips at night. Give a reward for referring a new employee with green values to the company.

These are all good ideas, but there are many others you or your staff can think up. It is always more productive if a group imagines the world of possibilities. It gets their creative juices going and generates enthusiasm for any program that is put in place.

It is of critical importance when implementing green policies and procedures that the top level of management leads by example. If the CEO turns off his or her power strip for electronics in the office before going home, it is more likely that everyone else will too. The same green rules and perks need to apply for everyone in the organization to realize success.

Mandating Behavior

Some businesses and organizations are forcing green behavior by their employees. This is less desirable for your business culture because achieving cooperation through voluntary and collaborative action results in more lasting behavioral changes. Nonetheless, some businesses have tried coercing behavior. Government entities, such as the City of San Francisco, have banned city departments from buying bottled water, including for water coolers, insisting that city employees drink city water to help stem global warming and save taxpayer money. In areas where the tap water is high quality, this can work. There is an enormous environmental impact in making, transporting, and disposing of the plastic bottles. Buy reusable water bottles only for staff that need to be on the go and first try to educate before you legislate. You may be surprised at how effectively it works.

A somewhat more controversial idea is to ban fragrances—perfumes and colognes—in the workplace. Employees who use fragrance can give their coworkers headaches. This can be a difficult policy to implement and police. Where do you stop? What about strong smelling hair products or hair spray? Some companies ban perfume and cologne but not other personal care products with fragrance. Any kind of ban can still send the message that a fragrance could affect someone's health and the indoor air quality of the building. Organizations that employ a person or persons with multiple chemical sensitivities may need to ban personal fragrances in order to keep them employed.

Easy Steps to Green

Following are six helpful tips to get you started greening your operation. Be sure to have a positive and Can Do attitude about making these changes—this is the creative and fun part of business. If you attack these changes with a positive spirit, you will have a good experience. There are no hard and fast rules to any of this, because it is a new area of innovation. Feel free to recycle ideas and build on what others have tried. There is nothing proprietary in these concepts. Have some fun boasting to your business colleagues about what your business or division is doing to make your organization more sustainable.

1. Develop your Organization's Green Values

In order to decide where to start with greening the operation of any organization, you must first understand the personality of the organization. Read the mission, vision, and values to see if there are any clues as to what is the most important. If the old mission didn't account for environmental responsibility or a Statement of Values for the organization does not exist, perhaps it is time to put some time and energy into revisiting these basic building blocks of any organizational structure (more about how to do this in Chapter 11). Some of the operational changes will then be obvious. For example, a grocery store should encourage its staff to eat organic food. An energy company could provide compact fluorescents to employees and subsidize energy audits. Start with the obvious then get more creative as you implement.

2. Hire a Sustainability Manager

Sustainability should be everyone's job, but in the beginning it helps to put someone in charge. This is becoming a career path for professionals who work across departments in an organization to inspire a new shade of corporate green. In the old days, green was assigned to the environmental engineers and compliance departments of companies that had reporting requirements for various polluting activities like smokestack or water pipe discharges. Today, a sustainability manager or director of sustainability is likely to be a general businessperson, who is charged with suggesting programs and ideas for greening the operation.

3. Set up Green Committees Organized Across Operational Functions

One of the best ways to get people excited about something is to assign them to solve a problem. This engages them completely in the process and helps to get their agreement. To successfully implement a green operations program tap the best, brightest, and most positive people in the organization and in each functional area. Use them as idea generators and cheerleaders. If you are going to take on a big task like becoming paperless, get a committee together to work on it that will be able to work well together and make its way through any problems or setbacks.

4. List and Prioritize Ideas

Much like a design charrette for green building, have a brainstorming meeting to come up with operation ideas that are green. Don't critique any idea, just record everything that is said and build on each other's ideas. It is best to have someone facilitate this process. Once you have a list of ideas, cull through it and prioritize, listing the easiest and least costly changes first. Don't fall into the trap of feeling the company must be instantly green and do everything at once. Set up a reasonable timeline, and implement a few things over a one-year period.

5. Institute a Green Procurement Program

Anytime the organization buys something, whether it's paper, copy toner, or coffee for the break room, have a policy in place to encourage green purchases. Soon it will be part of the culture and a habit for those making the purchases. Initially there may be resistance, because it will mean a little more work to find green vendor options and set up the relationship with them. It is human nature to want to use the same old tried-and-true vendors over and over. Consider first asking your current vendor for a green alternative and then switch if that isn't feasible.

6. Develop a Sustainability Performance Report

Once you have some green programs up and running, a sustainability report can help communicate your efforts to the entire company. Some publicly held corporations are making sustainability reports part of their annual communication to shareholders. The Global Reporting Initiative has developed specific guidelines to provide a framework for what to report and how to report it. Essentially, the report must say what is proposed, how it will be measured, and what progress has been made in accomplishing it. If, for example, a company wants to improve its environmental and social (ethical labor practices, diversity of the work force and philanthropic activities) performance, it should find a means to measure that performance and share it with stakeholders.

Even small companies can develop their own versions of a sustainability report with as much or as little detail as they want to disclose. It helps to demonstrate their interest and commitment to the environment and human rights issues. It can also communicate their various green initiatives to customers, vendors, employees, and the world. A report, even if it is found only on the company website, can enhance brand value and help build the organization's reputation. It is also a good way for prospective employees to understand what the organization is doing to be sustainable.

Chapter 8

Greening the Fleet—
Moving People and Product

According to *The Consumer's Guide to Effective Environmental Choices*, published by the Union of Concerned Scientists, the single most environmentally damaging consumer behavior is the use of cars, SUVs, and pickups. This isn't surprising. We are all guilty. Our love affair with driving and our need to move things from here to there causes toxic air pollution, smog, and greenhouse gas. Gas and oil spills as well as leaky vehicles are a major source of water pollution, as are the production of the vehicles and the petroleum to run them. So anything that we can do to help our employees drive less is an important step in environmental protection.

According to the U.S. Environmental Protection Agency's website (*www.epa.gov*), 35 billion gallons of diesel fuel is used to deliver goods by truck and rail each year, generating nearly 350 million tons of carbon dioxide (CO_2). Idling trucks and rail are responsible for about 20 percent of the CO_2 emissions. Idling means that they are sitting still and getting zero miles to the gallon but are powering heaters or air conditioners for driver sleeping or refrigerator units for the cargo. Unfortunately, fuel consumption for transportation directly correlates to the amount of emissions that pollute the air. It follows that reducing fuel consumption will cut greenhouse gas and smog emissions too.

Transportation is necessary for business. So critical is it, in fact, that we rarely see how much we are contributing to the problem. But every time you move people, materials, or products, you are creating further damage to the earth. On the other hand, this means that every day you have a new opportunity to be a part of the solution. Increasing oil prices seem to be creating a new and growing awareness about opportunities in green logistics. A tremendous amount of investment dollars are going into greener transportation alternatives, and we should see big progress in this area over the next ten to twenty years. But why wait? There are things your business can do right now to reduce the environmental impacts of transportation.

This chapter will give you several solutions you can implement immediately—simple things that you can try. Much of greening a business can be compared to an exercise program—anything that you can do is better than sitting on the couch doing nothing. Much like exercise, it is the small unglamorous things that will most improve your gas mileage and reduce your emissions. Exciting, yet uncomplicated, solutions are popping up around the globe.

Opportunity: Moving Employees and Customers

A few years ago, it was unheard of to worry about your employees and customers being able to afford the trip to your place of business. Now, if your business isn't convenient, a customer may choose not to spend the gas money needed to get there. There are some simple ways to encourage greener transportation. Not only will your customers save money, it will be easy for them to get to you. Each time a vehicle isn't used, there are fewer emissions, less petroleum needed, and better water quality for all of us. So start small.

Any kind of parking lot or ramp, whether it is for an office, plant, or store, has convenient parking and less-convenient parking. The company's top brass are often given the most convenient parking spots. How about changing the rules? This was mentioned in the previous chapter when discussing how to encourage your employees to be green, but don't forget the customer. It shouldn't be just the first or luckiest customers to arrive who get the best parking. To promote green transportation behavior, give the most convenient parking to those that drive the most energy-efficient vehicles. Create signs in the parking area to designate a green car parking zone. The zone can include electric vehicles, hybrid gas-electric, hydrogen, scooters, motorcycles, and any other kind of vehicle that has high gas mileage and low emissions.

If the parking lot is in the planning stages or in need of resurfacing, install electric cabling and plug-ins for electric vehicles to charge up. This is a new twist on an old idea from the cold, blustery Midwest plains during the winter. Apartment buildings in this part of the country had plug-in outdoor parking for cars to hook up their tank heaters when the temperature fell below zero. Residents paid a little more for those preferred spots and could sleep well knowing that their car will start on a cold winter morning. Given the limited range of totally electric vehicles, having a port in the parking lot where drivers can connect to a power source is a great perk.

One other simple, retro, idea is to install bike racks. As the cost of gasoline rises, more and more people are commuting on two wheels and need a safe place to leave their bicycles during the day. Providing an attractive bike rack or locked bike corral will be helpful to cyclists. Otherwise, provide bike lockers in an underground parking facility or the basement of the building as an incentive to arrive at work or shop via human-powered wheels. There are also new hybrid bicycles that are part human powered and part battery operated—they can even have a shell or covered cockpit to protect the rider from the elements in colder climates. Someone driving this kind of device might be more inclined to drive it to your business if you provide convenient and safe parking.

Car sharing, a short-term car rental arrangement, is a green transportation phenomenon that is catching on in metropolitan areas all over the United States. Members of a car-sharing program, such as Zipcar (*www.zipcar.com*), reserve a rental car for a specific short period of time, like an hour or two. There are locations or hubs where the vehicles are picked up and dropped off, so that the next person can rent it. Someone who normally takes public transportation but needs a car occasionally can use and pay for the car only when he is using it. One of the general tenets of green is that it's better to use than to own. A car-sharing arrangement gives you the use of the car without all of the costs and hassles of ownership. This reduces the amount of resources used, since one car is used by dozens or hundreds of people.

More on Car Sharing

For more information on car sharing, check out the Car Sharing Network website (*www.carsharing.net*). This website lists (with links) what car-sharing options are available in cities across the United States and Canada. If you need car-sharing facts to help convince your organization or employees to get involved with this resource-saving service, you'll find those here as well.

Locating a car-sharing hub on or near your property is another inexpensive way to help green the transportation of your business. Employees, customers, and neighborhood people can all benefit from your hub. The environment benefits too, because there are fewer cars on the road. The business benefits by providing access for people to run errands during the day or get to an appointment that is inaccessible by mass transit. You may even be able to realize revenue for the business by leasing a spot to a car-sharing company.

Another way to get employees out of their cars is to provide free or subsidized mass-transit passes. In addition to the direct environmental benefits, this also helps with overcrowding in parking lots. If employees don't want to use public transportation, carpooling is still a good way to wisely use resources. Set up a carpool matching service on your company intranet, and give a small cash incentive or free parking pass to carpoolers. Another timely idea is to give gas vouchers or a gas subsidy to carpoolers and drivers of high mileage vehicles. Likewise, encouraging the use of high-mileage vehicles is helpful. Consider giving employees a grant, loan, or cash bonus of $1,000 when they buy a gas-electric hybrid.

Hybrid Is the Way to Go

In my construction company we have a small fleet of Toyota Prius hybrids for employees who travel to various construction jobs during the day. Buying vehicles that get forty-five to fifty miles to the gallon was more cost efficient for the company than paying employees a mileage reimbursement—particularly as gasoline prices soared. After the cars have been used for two years, we offer them for sale at a discount to employees. We have a waiting list of employees who want to purchase the used cars. The employees who drive these cars love showing them off to clients and vendors. The car becomes a teaching tool. Employees have said that after their hybrid company car, they won't drive anything else. The cars also make a statement everywhere they go. Clients and subcontractors know that we care about our resource use and choose a car that spews fewer emissions into the atmosphere.

Purchase a fleet of vehicles that is the right size for a job. Size does matter, and bigger may be unnecessary. In my business, we finally realized that our maintenance technicians did not need SUVs, vans, or pickup trucks to do their jobs. They had plenty of room in a hatchback sedan: the Prius. For years we'd succumbed to the false idea that construction jobs required a large vehicle. We paid escalating fuel prices for fourteen to eighteen miles per gallon. Now our construction vehicles get at least two and a half times that mileage, and no one's job performance has been impacted.

Allowing employees to work from home, as mentioned in the previous chapter, is a green business answer. Telecommuting or teleworking is a big green win, because employees do not need to get in their car to get to work. Working from home doesn't work for companies where an employee's physical presence is required, but it can work in many more situations than it is currently allowed. Many businesses resist it because of fear. They fear losing control of the employee and they don't trust that the employee will work when he or she is out of sight.

My property management firm sent many employees home to telecommute in 2000, and the experience has been overwhelmingly positive. Yes, there have been a few rogue employees over the years who have been a problem, but they would have been a problem in the office too. We found that employees tend to work more productively, not less so, from home. In fact, they often have fewer distractions at home than in the office. They also tend to work longer hours on average, because there is no drive time and they tend to take a shorter lunch. They are the most loyal employees with the longest tenures. Most of our teleworkers have at least one day of face time each week in the main office. This helps keep a human connection and allows them time to open snail mail and maintain relationships with staff.

Since many of our staff work offsite, we can maintain a smaller physical office, which saves a tremendous amount of resources both in natural capital and ongoing heating, cooling, and lighting costs.

Four-day workweeks for staff who need to be physically in the office is also a good gas saving strategy. They work ten hours per day instead of the usual eight. Since commuting gas can cost some workers a much as an entire week's pay, allowing them to make the trip into the office one less day a week can be a big savings for them. Employees typically see the three-day weekend as a perk. The environment wins by less gas, emissions, and wear and tear on the roads. The business still has the benefits of staff working forty-hour weeks. If there is a need to cover office or shift hours of a typical five-day workweek, you can achieve this by rotating the staff through the week. As gas prices rise, many companies are experimenting with a four-day workweek.

Finally, you can use online meeting tools as a way to keep employees out of cars and airplanes yet maintain active connections with clients and fellow employees. The technology has come a long way in the past couple of years. Any size organization can use this tool with far-flung employees, customers, and potential customers. The web meeting tools are becoming more sophisticated and less expensive. Most online meeting tools can walk someone through a PowerPoint presentation in a web meeting, and many can be used for much more. Application sharing, shadowing, on-demand training, and polling of employees or customers are a few examples of what can be done remotely at very low prices.

Opportunity: Moving Product

Not only do we move people in businesses, but we move things. For thousands of years we've been moving products on foot and by boat, but since the Industrial Revolution and the invention of the carbon-powered engine, we increasingly move things around the world by air, sea, and land. Products sometimes travel not just once around the world but several times in their life cycle. As an illustration, iron ore is mined in northern Minnesota, shipped overseas to Asia where many auto parts are made, and then shipped back to the United States to make cars. The cars are then manufactured in Detroit and put on trucks to dealerships before they are shipped to other stores to satisfy consumers' color and options demands. Once a car has been used by a consumer in the United States, it may then be shipped once again to the other side of the globe for a second or third life in China or Indonesia. Such a process burns a huge amount of carbon and expels enormous quantities of greenhouse gases into the atmosphere. This is one of the downsides of our global economy.

Every business in our economy gets goods from somewhere else. The restaurateur sources coffee from South America, the office buys toner cartridges made in China, the clothing retailer sells jeans made in Vietnam. Transportation is involved in nearly every single transaction in our economy, yet we take it for granted. No matter how green we are, we rarely, if ever, think about how a product came to us. But a long list of environmental problems accompanies every kind of shipping.

All forms of shipping use fossil fuels and create greenhouse gases and other air pollutants:

> Gasoline and diesel trucks are fuel-sucking machines that emit the most greenhouse gases.

> Air shipping also produces a large amount of emissions and uses a tremendous amount of fuel.

> Rail is less polluting than airplanes or trucks but not always as convenient.

> Ocean transport and inland shipping are probably the most efficient, because water transportation has the best energy ratio per unit of transportation. But maritime shipping still produces greenhouse gases, and there are ballast water management issues, fuel spills, and leaks, let alone ships harming migrating marine life and destroying coral reefs.

No method of moving product is environmentally benign. If you ship materials or product regularly to sell or manufacture, it is well worth getting involved with a green cargo group to ensure you are moving the product in as efficient and clean a way as possible.

Business for Social Responsibility has a working group, the Clean Cargo Working Group, that is active in promoting sustainable product transportation. The group targets all modes of international transport and addresses environmental and social impacts of transporting goods. The group includes manufacturers, retailers, and carriers who discuss how to provide responsible transportation. The very existence of the group is a hopeful sign that this issue is being studied. Thus, joining the group, reading their reports, or finding a shipper that has signed on to be part of the Clean Cargo group would be a good starting point for greening your business's cargo.

As I've said before in this book, buy *local* materials and have the product made locally. Local has taken on new meaning since the economy has become global. Local can be defined as your city, state, or region, but it can also mean as far away as another state or even Canada. In both the United States and Canada, environmental regulations are fairly stringent and well enforced, so even if the product or raw material needs to travel some distance, there is some assurance that the transport is relatively clean. In a global economy, practically anything that doesn't travel half way around the world is considered local.

Another way to minimize transportation's negative effects on the environment is to reduce the size of products so more of the product can fit in a shipping container or truck, reducing the overall energy used to get it from here to there. Some liquid products, such as All Small and Mighty liquid laundry detergent, have been reformulated into a concentrate allowing for smaller bottles. This helps save resources in making the bottle, but it also conserves shipping energy. Even though the bottles are smaller, the same number of laundry loads can be washed as with the detergent stored in a bottle two to three times larger.

The electronics industry is also moving to reduce the size of electronic components. This can save raw materials and resources when shipped. In both examples, the customer gets the same use out of a smaller product, and the environment wins. This can be done with any number of consumer products.

A low-tech way of reducing the environmental effects of transportation is to make it a gimmick—deliver product via human power using no carbon at all. Some pizza businesses, coffee bean delivery services, and courier services do this already. Depending on climate, traffic, and urban density, this may be the preferred way to move product around. Other businesses, like UPS, are getting fleets of hybrid vehicles or are experimenting with electric vehicles and even hydrogen-powered fleets. Some companies are successfully using their earth-friendly transportation as a marketing advantage. There are taxicab companies in New York and Seattle that have gas-electric hybrid vehicles, and they market them specifically to attract customers.

Even the government has gotten into the green transportation act. As of the fall of 2007, the EPA's program, SmartWay Transportation Partnership, for rail and trucking fleets, is helping business access information on how to be greener. SmartWay also provides contacts to lenders, who offer loans to trucking companies to help pay for technologies that will save fuel and reduce pollution. Contracting with a shipper that appears as a SmartWay partner on the EPA website is one way of knowing they have the issue on their green radar screen.

Opportunity: Online Selling

E-commerce sales have increased by double digits over the past few years. Selling online is generally more environmentally friendly than from a bricks-and-mortar location. Yes, large e-commerce operations still need an office and a warehouse, but smaller storefronts can use a decentralized telecommuting staff and subcontracted fulfillment houses to warehouse and ship their product. Fewer buildings to build, heat, cool, and power saves energy and resources. It also saves the financial resources of the online retailer because the company doesn't have to financially support the real estate as do its brick-and-mortar cousins.

It is also better for the environment if consumers stay at home shopping on their computers instead of driving around in their cars. The product still needs to be delivered to their door by a gas-using, emission-excreting truck. But remember that the truck is presumably on an efficiently planned route, dropping off many packages. This is many times more efficient than all those consumers getting in their vehicles and driving to pick up a single item.

Transportation of online products can still be a problem for the environment, but e-retailers can minimize the impact. One way to do this if you're an e-tailer is to give shoppers an incentive to buy several products at once. This will cut down on the number of trips your delivery truck needs to make. Retailers and fulfillment houses can set up systems to hold product until a full order is assembled. Rarely does someone really need the product shipped overnight. Encourage ground transportation. While faster, air transportation uses many times the amount of fuel as a large truck. It is possible to structure the pricing of your products to reward more environmentally friendly shipping. For instance, you can add an extra charge for air transport.

An e-retailer can also be green by making sure to contract only with shippers that are making an effort to green their fleet of delivery trucks. When hiring a shipper, find out if the company has a green logistics program. If it doesn't, find a shipper that does and is willing to tell you about its program. Be sure to let your customer know about your efforts to get the product to them in an earth-friendly manner.

The environmental downside of e-commerce is the cost to businesses, consumers, and society of business e-mail spam. Spam accounts for 80 to 95 percent of the e-mail traffic in the world today. Believe it or not, besides being irritating spam has an environmental cost. All told, millions of hours of productivity are lost due to spam. Even with antispam software, employees often must wade through hundreds of annoying and offending e-mail messages to get to a couple of legitimate e-mails in their inbox. Spam slows down the entire Internet by clogging servers around the world. Computers become slower, and equipment becomes obsolete faster, as new hardware is installed to handle the congestion. In the end, more electronic debris is added to the environmental pile, because companies and individuals strive to avoid the spam clog. So if you are going to sell product online, do not use spam e-mail.

Opportunity: Carbon Neutrality

Carbon-powered engines still power most of our transportation. It is disturbing to realize that no matter how much you reduce driving or how careful you are about the transportation vendors you use, your business will still be adding greenhouse gases to the atmosphere. An up-and-coming way to deal with inevitable tail-pipe emissions is to purchase carbon offsets. Offset money goes to ongoing projects run by organizations capable of reducing the amount of greenhouse gases being produced. Projects include those that absorb or sequester carbon from the air—for example, tree-planting projects in Rivas, Nicaragua where the nonprofit Carbon Fund (*www.carbonfund.org*) is reforesting an area larger than Central Park and will sequester 150,000 metric tons of carbon dioxide emissions. Renewable energy programs like wind turbines at the Garwin McNeilus Wind Farm in Dodge Center, Minnesota, that don't produce carbon emissions are also common and can be purchased from Terrapass (*www.terrapass.com*). Offsets are priced at $2–$30 per ton of carbon or carbon dioxide equivalents (to address other greenhouse gases besides carbon dioxide). A polluter can pay someone else not to pollute or to repair damage from greenhouse gases somewhere else in the world, thereby, in a sense, canceling out his or her own organization's pollution.

The Kyoto Protocol set up a regulated cap-and-trade system for carbon emissions. If a participating entity emits above its cap, then it can trade for carbon offsets. So far, in the United States there are only voluntary carbon trading and carbon offset programs, and neither are regulated. They are still controversial, in part because they are not regulated. There is a line of thought that companies should just all reduce emissions, not trade for them, but carbon credits will no doubt be part of the market mechanism that helps us transition away from a carbon-based economy. Carbon credits, voluntary or regulated, are a way for small and medium-sized companies concerned about their contribution to climate change to commit to being as carbon neutral as possible.

Figuring out how to offset carbon for transportation doesn't need to be complicated. For starters you can make a simple calculation using one of the many carbon footprint websites. If you have a sales force that flies around the country, you can use an online calculator to figure out the average greenhouse gases per salesperson per year. Then you can purchase offsets for that one line item of expense on your budget. If you have a service crew in vehicles, you can estimate the amount of offsets you need per average vehicle miles driven in a month or year, depending on the car's efficiency. For example, a hybrid vehicle would require less in offsets than a standard gas-powered vehicle. To calculate offsets for product transportation and other more complicated functions, you may want to contact an environmental consulting firm or an offset provider.

Some businesses are leery about getting involved in the voluntary carbon offset market because they don't know which providers to trust—there are no uniformly recognized standards for carbon offsets yet, and new providers crop up daily. This doesn't mean that there isn't a program out there for your business. Be smart when investigating the possibilities. A credible offset provider, whether it is protecting forests or creating renewable technologies, should be able to give you concrete assurance that its reductions in greenhouse gases are measurable and verifiable. Be sure to do thorough due diligence and check carefully into the background of the company and offset projects. Make sure they are legitimate and effective before you make a commitment. Legitimate offset organizations and their specific offset programs have been verified by a third-party verification bodies. To help you sort out if your money is going to verifiable projects, ask the offset provider for proof from the auditing firm. Ecobusinesslinks.com provides a carbon offset directory listing many of the providers along with their projects and comparison pricing. Also make sure that the provider's projects align with your company's interests, goals, and values. Perhaps you want your dollars to fund projects in your local area rather than a hemisphere away. If so, finding a provider that is close to home should be a priority.

While some say that businesses should not be allowed to buy their way out of polluting, others believe that doing something is better than doing nothing in the midst of climate change. This is true especially since technology has yet to make it possible to completely eliminate carbon from the supply chain when producing a product or providing a service.

The carbon trading system is young and still has its flaws. Nonetheless, it is still worth investigating if your organization is trying to find some way to reduce its greenhouse gases. The first step is to reduce the amount of carbon your business emits through the opportunities discussed in this and previous chapters. Once your carbon footprint is as small as possible through efficiency and conservation, consider reducing the remaining carbon emissions by purchasing carbon credits through a reputable provider.

Easy Steps to Green

The secret to greening your business's transportation is doing lots of little things that add up to something big. There are no easy single steps. It is more about keeping tires inflated to the proper PSI than it is about a new and exciting technology. The following steps will help you get in gear and begin to think about how your business can structure a green logistics program. As with so many other greening initiatives, both the planet and the business's bottom line will benefit. Reductions in fuel have a direct correlation to reductions in cost and greenhouse gases. Start small then add the sexier programs as your time, culture, and money permit.

1. Identify a Green Logistics Strategy

Make a list of all logistical events for your company. Do you move products in or out? Do you need to get employees or customers to your location? Or do you need to move employees to your customers? Then, quantify these logistics. You can improve what you measure. List the costs to the business associated with each event, like direct expenses for amount spent on fuel, vehicle miles, or shipping costs. Also list the indirect costs to the environment in emissions and deferred costs of wear and tear on your equipment or parking area. Choose to concentrate on a couple of these indicators that are the most meaningful to your staff. Once you have a baseline, brainstorm the ways to reduce the direct costs first. Then tackle the indirect costs.

2. Reduce Carbon Use with Incremental Small Practices

Start changing your practices with small policies before investing big dollars. Educate the vehicle drivers in your company to stay below sixty miles per hour on the highway. Train them to avoid rapid acceleration and braking to save fuel and emissions. Sponsor a monthly contest to reward the driver with the best fuel efficiency. Institute a "no idle" policy for all fleet vehicles. Identify the shortest routes for drivers, and monitor tire pressure for the proper pounds per square inch.

If you subcontract your shipping, find a company that understands green logistics and has made some demonstrable progress in greening its fleet. If you ship internationally, assign someone to monitor or join the Clean Cargo Working Group, so that your firm can be kept up-to-date on global green logistics progress.

3. Launch a Telecommuting Program

In nearly every organization there are people who could be sent home to work, saving precious square feet of office space and reducing the number of cars on the road. To begin a telecommuting or teleworking program, choose the right positions and the most self-motivated employees. Jobs requiring researching, writing, or number crunching don't necessarily need to be in the office daily and may have fewer interruptions at home. Choose employees who have expressed a desire to work from home and who have shown that they are organized, independent, and productive. Give the teleworker the right tools to work from home, such as a secure online connection to the office and a printer-fax-scanner combination. Be explicit about your expectations of the employees. Give them specific written job duties, work hours (or number of hours you expect them to work per day), and tell them the amount of office face time you expect. Try it with one or two employees at first to get the kinks out before you commit to a larger program.

4. Consider Carbon Offsets for What Cannot be Improved Further

No matter how much you have reduced your fuel and emission costs and consumption, you are still polluting and burning nonrenewable fuels. Green technology hasn't yet caught up to our earth-friendly needs. Until it does, consider a carbon offset program for what you cannot eliminate through conservation, retraining, and retrofitting. You can always start out with a higher proportion of offsets, then decrease them as your tangible reductions of greening your transportation are realized. Find a consultant who provides climate services to sort out whether carbon offsets are right for your company. Environmental services and large accounting firms sometimes offer this expertise. Or you can contact the carbon offset firms directly to find the right fit for your company's goals and values.

Chapter 9

Greening the Product— the Holy Grail

As you can see, there are many ways to green a business. Greening a building can save money and resources, so it is becoming more mainstream. Greening the operation responds to the need to create an eco-sensitive business culture that can recruit and retain loyal employees. It also results in a savings of money and resource. But the real moneymaking opportunity—the green home run— lies in producing green products and services. This is the Holy Grail of green. Green products and services are born to fulfill an unmet need. Creating a green product or service is the most creative, fulfilling, and exciting green play that a business can make.

A green product does less harm to the environment. Of course, as you now know, there is no such thing as a perfectly green, human-made product. All products do some harm to the environment either in the extraction of the materials, the manufacturing process, the transporting, the use, or the disposal. Even a renewable solar energy system needs metals and other materials from the earth to make the panels that collect the free sunshine. It's a better, but still not perfectly green, product. A perfectly green product would emulate something found in nature, where it is created, used, and disposed of, all the while keeping a perfect balance within the ecosystem.

Learn from the Worms

Worm composting is a good example of a natural cycle at work. Worms get their nutrition from leaves on the forest floor, clean up the floor, and poop out nutritious compost creating new nutrients or food to grow new plants. Once the plants grow they drop leaves on the forest floor starting the perfect cycle all over again. In nature, nothing is ever wasted or used up. Waste from one organism is food for another and so it goes.

The $500 billion question is, how can you make your products and services more closely emulate nature so that you don't use up your resources? There is an old adage among farmers: "Don't eat your seed corn." In other words, leave some seed to replant or you won't have a crop the following year. The current methods we use to produce products and services create the real possibility that we will leave nothing to replant. If we use every last resource there will be nothing to replenish our supply. It's true you may never have a perfectly green product. Still, you can move along the continuum from brown to greener products, just as people are changing their behavior from brown to green. It is not a simple task, but in the past few years there has been a movement to greener products. As our resources have become more expensive, innovators have focused their attention on green design.

Any product or service can be made more earth friendly. It can happen in the product design stage, such as when the first gas-electric hybrid car was conceived. It can also occur when a company redesigns a current product, like light bulb manufacturers deciding to redesign the light bulb as a small, tubular fluorescent bulb capable of generating the same amount of lumens with many times less energy use. Or companies can accomplish greening at any link in the product or service supply chain. You also have opportunities to green products by paying attention to what they become after their use. A few years back a company made plastic containers from plant polymers, which can decompose. This was a big improvement on the containers manufactured from petroleum, which harm the environment after their useful life.

Opportunity: Product Trends

Organic food was one of the first consumer products to be widely defined and certified as green. There are universally accepted standards that define organic as creating trust with consumers and fueling tremendous growth in that market segment. Organic food has become an introductory green product for consumers.

Once consumers start buying it, they look for other products labeled organic, natural, or green. Their perspective transforms, and they associate organic with quality, goodness, and health. The organic foods market has realized incredible growth over the past decade. It doesn't matter that consumers may not fully appreciate the breadth of the environmental benefits of organic foods, including healthy soil, less-polluted water, and a healthier ecosystem. And it hasn't seemed to matter much that organic foods can be 5–20 percent more expensive than nonorganic foods. A growing segment of the population will buy organic to give their family the very best. Fortunately, that buying behavior is spilling over to other related green product markets. For instance, organic cotton baby clothes and baby bedding are growing trends. Similarly, organic cotton and other natural fibers for every kind of clothing are gaining market share.

Another result from the success of organics is the growth of the natural personal-care market. Consumers have become more aware about what they are putting *in* their bodies by eating organics. The natural next step is for them to become aware of what they are putting *on* their bodies. Consumers now question the ingredients in their lotions, makeup, soap, shampoo, and other personal-care products. Green personal-care products using less chemicals and more natural formulations are now increasing in visibility and market share.

Consumers care deeply about their family pets. The organics phenomenon has extended into the pet care industry, with human-quality organic and all-natural pet foods, dog chews, treats, toys, and less-toxic grooming products.

This same phenomenon is beginning in other industries. The green building boom is a good example. In the past few years, the industry has developed standards to define green building. There are third-party certifying entities that authenticate the standards that must be met. The standards give consumers the assurance they need to buy green-related houses and are pushing this sector over the tipping point. Due to the green building push and the high cost of energy, consumers are also learning to be energy efficient, buying compact fluorescent light bulbs and power strips to turn off electronics. They are starting to pay attention to their air quality by buying better furnace filters, less-toxic paints, and nontoxic cleaning products. The convergence of information about organics and green building has inspired consumer green product interest in home décor—furniture and accessories that are all natural, recycled, reclaimed, or less toxic are becoming popular.

There are just as many opportunities to green service-oriented businesses as consumer-product businesses. My property management firm was able to green its services by using green service providers for functions such as organic lawn maintenance, less-toxic cleaning services, and integrated pest management.

Real estate firms are greening their services by listing and selling green homes. A few insurance companies are greening their services by providing a green insurance product that gives discounts to green buildings. Hair salons are offering chemical-free services. Some restaurants and bars are serving mostly local and organic food and drinks. It is possible to add green offerings to just about any service business. So far, many are following the same trends as green products in the home, food, car, and energy markets. A world of green opportunity lies ahead in the service sector, waiting to be discovered.

We have to start somewhere. Track product and service trends to see what fits your own business. But the true green challenge is to make any old, run-of-the-mill product or service green. How do you green a mattress, dinnerware, or a dentist office? So far, green products visually stand out. They look different from traditional products—many look more natural, meaning earthy or earth-toned in color. But is that what consumers really want? The majority of consumers want products they can recognize. The ultimate challenge is to create products that are green in their very DNA but look, feel, behave, and cost the same as their less-green counterparts. The quest to do this is the search for the Holy Grail.

Opportunity: Reinvention

It isn't that we are doing things so wrong—it's that we have the capability to do things so much better. We, as a species, can imagine, create, and innovate to improve on what has been done before us. With this ability, we can reinvent our world in a cleaner and greener way. Clean technology is one of the catchall phrases for this reinvention of commerce. Billions of investment dollars are going into clean tech. Experts say that clean tech will be bigger than the dollars that flowed into new companies and ideas in the dot-com era of the late 1990s. It includes renewable energy technologies, breakthroughs in cleaner transportation, clean water innovations, and green chemistry. In short, green tech includes almost everything that is being designed today with the environment in mind.

Green chemistry, or sustainable chemistry, is redesigning many of the products we commonly use. It focuses on minimizing the hazard of any chemical used to make products. Some of the principles of green chemistry include:

> Preventing waste so there are no hazardous substances to clean up

> Designing products and substances that are effective but have little or no toxicity (for instance, cleaning products and low-VOC paints)

> Using renewable raw materials from agriculture rather than fossil fuels, such as plastics made from soy or corn stocks and not petroleum

> Designing products so they degrade into innocuous substances after their use, avoiding waste left to accumulate in the environ-

ment (for instance, biobased plastic bags or containers that are composted and disappear)

Other terms for environmentally sound product and service reinvention are *design for the environment*, *green design*, and *eco-design*. When social and economic impacts are added to the environmental design life cycle considerations, the approach is called *design for sustainability*. This approach is still in the early stages of defining itself. Some design firms work as hired guns for companies, specializing in designing green products wishes. There are also green designers on the staff of major manufactures such as Honda, Apple, and Sony. Green design is a growing field, staffed with the best and brightest the world has to offer.

Another movement of green reinvention is biomimicry or bionics, as it is called in Europe. Biomimicry is a new science that studies nature and then takes inspiration from it to create sustainable solutions. Since nature is the best engineer and has figured out after 3.8 billion years of experimenting what works and what doesn't, scientists ask how nature would solve the problem. If we can discover how animals, plants, and microbes are designed, we can figure out how we should more effectively design what we create.

Janine Benyus was one of the first to apply this line of reasoning in her 1997 book, *Biomimicry: Innovation Inspired by Nature*. Up to this point in human history, we have made things by cutting away at a natural resource, heating it, and then manipulating it into a form requiring an enormous expenditure of energy. All this requires an enormous expenditure of energy. On the other hand, biomimicry uses design and engineering to mimic what happens in nature, sometimes on a nanoscale, requiring much less energy.

For example, humans can learn from red seaweed how to repel bacteria rather than kill it. We can create an antibiotic that minimizes bacterial resistance. Or we can mimic the red abalone shell structure that is both lightweight and remarkably strong to design and manufacture a new lightweight building material. As biology and nanotechnology become more sophisticated, we will see more and more products designed with biomimicry. If this seems too far-fetched to apply to your own product or service, here are some simple eco-design elements that can be easily applied when updating a product or designing something new:

Design a service, not a product. What consumers really want is the utility from a product. They don't necessarily want the actual thing. Music downloads are an excellent example. If consumers really wanted the object in which the music or video was packaged, we might still have vinyl records. Music download businesses such as iTunes are selling the experience of music, which can be played and replayed on an MP3 player. Car sharing is another good example of enjoying utility rather than the object. Consumers have use of the car for an hour at a time. When they have finished with their short-term use, someone else uses the car, spreading the resource costs over many people.

My company used this principle regarding our paperless application for the property management industry. Rather than producing and selling the application on discs, which the clients must load on their hard drives, we sell the use of the application as an application service provider (ASP). For a monthly fee, other management firms can tap into our Internet-enabled program to run their firm and manage property without having to put the cash up front to buy or build an application. We sell, or more accurately, rent, the utility to those who want to use it.

Design products to be more durable. Durability reduces resource use, because products don't need to be replaced as often. To give a product staying power, make it upgradeable. Computers, phones, or appliances can be designed to be upgraded with a new chip or software, rather than replacing the CPU, screen, and printer every few years.

Design for disassembly. A newer discipline in green product innovations is designing products so that everything can be quickly and easily pulled apart for reuse. This ability to easily dismantle for reuse keeps previously extracted resources circulating around the planet forever, rather than dead-ending in our landfills. Unfortunately, this sounds easier than it is in practice. Typically, recycling has involved shredding used materials such as plastic milk jugs and newspapers—it's low tech and quick. On the other hand, disassembly requires taking each component apart, so the initial product design needs to take this into account. Parts must be removed without being damaged, and materials need to be easily separated: plastics from metals, different types of plastics from each other, and hazardous materials from the rest. The disassembly needs to be easy and fast for the reuse or remanufacturing to be cost effective.

Even so, it is being done in certain product lines. Humanscale, a maker of ergonomic office products, designs high-performance desk chairs with disassembly and reuse in mind. Their Freedom chair is made with 132 parts, compared to their competitor's 278 parts. There are fewer pieces to remove when recycling. Additionally, Humanscale uses aluminum whenever possible because it never degrades and can be reused over and over again. About 85 percent of all materials in Humanscale products are recycled.

Designing for disassembly is possible and profitable. Humanscale accounts for approximately 10 percent of the high-performance desk chair market and has won numerous awards for its designs.

Design smaller products. Using less of any material when designing a product can also make it more sustainable. It may seem obvious that a smaller product uses fewer raw materials, but perhaps not so obvious is the savings in transportation costs. Transporting a smaller and lighter product equals less fuel and emissions.

Design to use low-embodied energy materials. Embodied energy refers to the amount of energy needed to manufacture and supply to the consumer a product or service. Think of it as the true energy cost of a product. If you analyze the amount of the embodied energy for a product or service, it helps you to understand where savings can be made in the supply chain. It also can inform your material selection. Typically, resources that are extracted from the earth will have a higher embodied energy than things grown on the surface of the earth.

Design using renewable materials. A product is more sustainable if it is made using renewable materials, such as plant fibers, or with renewable energy, such as wind or solar power. A product is less sustainable if made with materials extracted from the earth's crust. You must use caution, however, to make sure an agricultural product has not replaced an entire natural ecosystem. Proper land-management practice requires that an assessment be made to determine if the area needed to grow the product is environmentally favorable. Unfortunately, there are plenty of instances around the world where perfectly good forests are being cut down to feed the growing, green demand for bamboo and organic cotton. One environmental mistake is being traded for another. The goal must be sustainability within the entire ecosystem. The lesson is to use renewable materials when producing a product, but don't destroy other renewable materials to achieve such production.

Design using recycled materials. Products that are designed to be manufactured from recycled materials are often the better choice. One idea is to use the scrap materials from your own factory floor, such as recycling sawdust or fabric scraps, to create other products. This is a good start, but too many manufacturers stop there. An even better environmental practice would be to use scraps or garbage from other manufacturers as well. You can earn an extra green point for using recycled materials high in postconsumer content.

Design for sex appeal and hip factor. There is no reason that sustainable products need to look any different than their traditional counterparts. Green products need to look, feel, and function like other products that are on the market. In fact, green products can push the boundaries of design not only in their ability to protect the planet, but also to enhance our visual world as well. I call this the cool factor, and it needs to be an integral part of the design outcome for green products.

Opportunity: Life Cycle Assessment

Products have historically been designed based on cradle-to-grave use. Materials are extracted and shipped to a manufacturer where they are formed into a product. The product is then shipped to another destination, where it is stored and eventually sold. The product then is in the hands of the consumer until the end of its "useful life," when it is sent to a landfill to decay. The problem with this kind of product life cycle is that many resources, including the raw materials and the energy expended during this process, are removed from the earth, burned, and expelled into the atmosphere as a greenhouse gas. If not burned, the product lives out its life in a county dump or landfill. This system is inefficient and wasteful.

Instead, look at green design opportunities to build a sustainable life cycle. In other words, design products that either go back into nature, are reborn in the natural ecosystem, or are disassembled and reborn in the industrial ecosystem as other products. This is a sustainable life cycle. It is the preferred, green design goal—birth to rebirth rather than birth to death. In 2002, Michael Braungart, a German chemist, and William McDonough, an architect, published *Cradle to Cradle: Remaking the Way We Make Things*, which calls for just this kind of transformation in design and industry.

As with most great concepts, the devil is in the details. How do you make the quantum leap from discarding products and filling landfills, oceans, and skies to one of an ecological nirvana? Most businesses in the United States are small with limited financial resources and cannot afford to ponder this design issue or begin solving it. Even large businesses see this as a sea change that they may not be able to navigate. Will the redesigned products be too expensive? Do you have the technology and know-how? Do consumers want cradle-to-cradle products? You must think backward from the end of your product; picture what it can be with no limitations.

Many breakthrough ideas in this area are already percolating. Renewable energy and hydrogen-powered homes and hydrogen fuel cell cars are in the prototype phases. The only byproduct from hydrogen-based systems is water. Recycled plastic food containers by SmartCycle are being remade into recycled plastic food containers, keeping the industrial nutrient in a loop of continuous manufacturing. The Corona Solar Lamp is a solar-powered outdoor lighting system that contains a photovoltaic cell, capturing sunlight to power LED lights. There are no glues or fasteners used to hold it together, so disassembly and recycling are quick and easy. These innovations exist, so there is hope that we can redesign the human-made world.

Life cycle assessment (LCA) is one tool that we can use to begin this redesign process. It is a holistic measure of the lifetime environmental impact of a product or service. The goal of LCA is to find a way to produce, move, use, and dispose of a product in a way that causes the least environmental damage. LCA is a process that is limited by our current understanding and quantitative information about environmental goods and evils. So far, it is being used sparingly by business. It can be complicated, time consuming, and expensive. Currently, it can cost hundreds of thousands of dollars to complete an LCA on a very complicated product.

When a full LCA is not feasible, standard life cycle indicators can be found for some products and processes, taking into account considerations like global climate change, human toxicity, ozone depletion, and impact on natural resources. You can compare these indicators with normalized indicators for products to get ideas for how to make environmental improvements to existing brands or businesses. One such simplified system is Eco-Indicator 99, which uses a simple set of inventory tables and impact data to give a basic assessment. SimaPro, another software program that is quick and easy to use, allows an experienced user to develop his or her own impact scores. Designers, product managers, and brand managers can easily use the programs to prioritize green design options.

Another breakthrough tool is product take-back programs. Companies that make or sell products are responsible for taking the product or part of the product back when the consumer is done with it. Parts of Europe and Japan require companies to take back certain items, such as bulky packaging and toxic materials, to keep that type of material out of the country's waste systems. In the United States, car batteries are one of the few examples of true take-back laws on the books. If we are truly moving toward a cradle-to-cradle economy, companies could start to implement voluntary take-back programs for products that have a high recycling value, like cars or electronics. The concept will make the most sense for business when products are designed for quick and easy disassembly and the cost of raw materials is more than the cost of repurposed materials.

Ethical Sourcing

Some companies are making the move to ensure that their products are made using sustainable practices and that their workers are treated fairly. This movement, called ethical sourcing, is bubbling up in supply-chain management around the world and has its roots in corporate social responsibility and reputation. Brands and companies (and their consumers) have been hammered by damaging incidents of mercury in lipstick, lead in toys, and food labeled organic that really isn't organic. Now that manufacturing is global rather than local, it's harder to keep an eye on the operation. Global commerce has made it difficult to ensure that suppliers are making products properly, which is why ethical and green supply-chain management is becoming a hot topic. Trusting the supply chain to keep products safe for consumption is difficult enough. Now we must ensure that products are environmentally benign and made in an ethical way.

One way to help ensure that products are being made responsibly and ethically is to create universally accepted standards that set the bar for what makes a product environmentally responsible. Perhaps one day there will be an agreement on social and environmental standards worldwide for products so that suppliers can comply. In a perfect world this would include standards for the entire supply chain, including mining, shipping, manufacturing, and disposal. Until then there is no need to struggle alone with this complicated issue. Worldwide conferences periodically convene to discuss ethical sourcing. Any business can attend to find contacts and new ideas for keeping tabs on subcontracted work in this country and abroad. In this relatively new world of global sourcing, the best we can do is to keep the discussion going so that we can find effective and affordable solutions.

Smaller companies that don't wield the power of a retail or brand giant have used guerrilla tactics to ensure that their supply chain is clean and green. They make surprise visits to manufacturers, growers, and miners of raw materials to ascertain whether those suppliers are meeting environmental and health standards. Some conscientious entrepreneurs will travel half way around the world many times a year to teach the employees of their subcontractors how to incorporate more sustainable practices on farm fields or in factories. They nurture personal relationships with their suppliers so that they can feel confident about the practices and materials used to make their products. This will continue to be one of the biggest greening challenges in the global economy—how to manage continuous oversight in the face of travel, language, and cultural barriers.

Carbon Offsets

We discussed carbon offsets earlier in the chapter on transportation. They can also be an effective tool for offsetting the greenhouse gases produced in raw material extraction and manufacturing. Even if a manufacturing plant is powered with renewable energy technologies, extraction of raw materials, including mining, farming, and logging, still produces greenhouse gases. Logging, in particular, can contribute to climate change, because it reduces the number of trees that are capable of absorbing greenhouse gases.

To get started with a carbon-offset program, first measure your overall CO_2 emissions for products, including their transportation. Once you have the baseline, you can identify areas to improve or offset. You can analyze or balance reductions according to your business's overall sustainability goals, carbon reduction goals, and financial goals. Some businesses are using carbon emission inventories to identify where they can shorten the supply chain, thereby reducing energy consumption and saving money. Recognize that an overall climate strategy is an iterative process that needs to be honed and adjusted continuously as information and technologies advance.

Opportunity: Environmental and Social Standards

Currently there are no product standards or certification programs for most green product categories. The green product frontier is the Wild West, where claims are often made with no backing, facts are exaggerated, and both the business and the consumer must beware. With few certification programs or third-party verification systems in place, businesses run the risk of selling or manufacturing products that are toxic, harmful, or unethically made. Sustainable standards, if they existed, would account for the three important elements of well-being: environmental, social, and economic. The upside of well-developed and accepted standards for business is more revenue and sales in more green-product categories. Retailers will carry products they know have been certified green and won't come back to bite them. Consumers will buy green products they know they can trust as long as it is price competitive and they perform as well as traditional products. It is a win-win proposition.

Eventually there will be more certification programs like the USDA Organic Certification in the United States, which gave farmers, grocers, and consumers universally accepted standards with common language and good rules. But it may be a while. A credible green product or service standards program must have a set of stringent but attainable and universally accepted standards. It also must be transparent, with criteria verifiable by third parties. This is where it gets complicated, since there are millions of products, processes and suppliers around the globe. Who has the capability to properly inspect and certify that each company is complying with the standards? Even if there is third-party certification, as with organic food, how do we keep graft and bribes out of the loop?

While there is nothing yet as advanced and comprehensive as the certified organic label for most green products, some certification programs do exist and are becoming more widely accepted. For instance:

> U.S. Green Building Council LEED certification for green buildings

> Green Seal for green cleaning solutions

> The Forest Stewardship Council for wood products

There are also some international approaches to sustainable standards that encompass environmental and social impacts of production. These programs are good benchmarks if you are searching for a way to green your product line and improve your company's corporate social responsibility grade.

The International Organization for Standardization (ISO) is a good place to start. The ISO 14000 series of environmental standards includes environmental management systems, environmental auditing, life cycle assessment (LCA) methodology, and environmental labeling. The more recently developed ISO 26000 series is an initiative that includes both environmental and socially sustainable voluntary guidelines. The United Nations Global Compact (UNGC) is another good starting point with principles that cover human rights, ethical and fair labor standards, environment stewardship, and anticorruption. There are also a number of governmental and quasi-governmental initiatives to promote responsible products. The Eco-label program of the European Union and Environmental Choice program of Canada are widely accepted government-run programs that encourage environmentally sound products. In both programs companies pay a fee for the certification process.

All of these programs have weaknesses and are not yet perfectly adaptable for every business, but reviewing the various standards is a good starting point for a business wishing to improve upon or create green products. Standards and certification programs will help make green products more credible and, ultimately, more profitable.

Easy Steps to Green

Designing products and services with sustainability in mind can boggle the mind, but it's also invigorating If you have a design staff, this is an exciting challenge to give them. Or you may want to hire some people who have green design expertise. But if you are a smaller business or organization, this might seem beyond your reach. Don't give up! It is simpler than it sounds. Here are some steps that can help you realize a new green design dream, no matter your business's size or budget.

1. Start Small

The first step is to set measurable goals for environmental changes. Start by tracking energy use for every link in your supply chain—energy use is the low-hanging fruit of sustainability strategies. Energy use or carbon emissions are the things that make the most environmental impacts. Greenhouse gases, climate change, air and water pollution, smog, resource depletion, and toxicity all lead back to the amount of energy expended to make, move, use, and dispose of a product. Measure energy use at a per-product level or some other easily understandable unit. Use an hourly billing unit if it is a service business. Then identify areas where you can shorten your supply chain to reduce energy use.

Research your supply chain. Find out where the raw materials originated. You can discover a surprising amount of information by doing an Internet search based on the country and region where the products were mined or farmed. Ask the obvious questions: "Where did this come from?" and "Why there?" Keep asking your suppliers until you get answers that make sense. You want to make sure that your materials were obtained legally and that the extraction or growing practices are in line with your environmental values and those you claim for the product.

2. Set the Bar

If there are no standards or certification programs for your product or service, develop your own for your business and suppliers to follow. The bar needs to be higher than just bare legal compliance but not so high that it isn't cost feasible. Green products need to be authentically green and affordable to most consumers. This is still a difficult combination. You may not develop the perfect set of environmental standards, but you will have a good starting point. Stay committed to continuously improving the standards as green technologies advance. Don't forget social standards. You may think that sweatshop labor went out with the last century, but in many places that's not the case. It's more important than ever to eliminate forced and compulsory labor, child labor, and discrimination in the workplace worldwide.

3. Assemble a Design Team

Do not try to go it alone when designing green products or standards. There are people in academia, industry, and environmental nonprofits who are all interested in making products greener and more sustainable. Some of the best minds in the world are working on this problem. Make some calls and assemble a team. The first place to call is your local university. There may be green design interns just waiting to get their hands on a real, live design problem. You may also be able to interest a professor or retired professor into joining your team. Also, check with your local environmental nonprofit organizations to see if anyone is doing work on either product standards or green design. Contact green design firms around the country or the world to find out how they work and what they would charge to work on your design problem.

Another possibility is to collaborate with other businesses in your industry to work on the design challenge. It may seem counterintuitive, but designing by mimicking nature or by using less energy is really an industry-wide challenge. So get your entire industry involved through a trade association or professional organization. Searching for the Holy Grail of green products will take an army of people, and the monetary reward of finding it will certainly be enough to go around.

4. Assemble a Supply-Chain Team

The best way to find solutions to a shorter, greener, and more ethical supply chain is through collaboration. Form a virtual multidisciplinary team with a raw materials provider, a manufacturer, a shipper, a retailer, and an end user for each product line. Include environmentalists with supply chain or standards experience to hold your feet to the fire on the more difficult environmental issues. Ask the team to come up with ongoing solutions for cutting energy use, reducing the carbon footprint, reducing toxicity, and improving social standards for workers at every stage in the supply chain.

Supply-chain management for service businesses is also important. I was able to achieve this in my property management business by coming up with a list of green criteria for our service subcontractors. The painting firms needed to use low-VOC paints, and the carpet layers needed to give us a recycled option and needed to recycle used carpets. We required the lawn vendors to provide an organic option of weed and feed. The cleaning and pest control subs must use less-toxic product alternatives. Managing our service supply chain with an eye for earth friendliness achieved two things: It made our services more in line with our business values, and it brought an awareness to our subcontractors about how they could green their services. They developed a new green practice within their operation that they could then sell to other firms. If you are breaking new ground, assemble a team of subcontractors and environmentalists to come up with ideas to green your service supply chain.

5. Find the Money

Don't let the shortage of money keep you from acting on an innovative green product or service idea. Investment capital is flooding into new, good green ideas because investors understand that green equals *green,* that is, money. Investors know that there is a fundamental cultural and economic shift occurring that favors the environment. Money is available for the right products and services. Private investors, angels, equity firms, and venture capitalists are all searching for the right green plays and are willing to invest to make them happen.

Remember, it's okay to do only one thing green that fits your business budget. Don't try to do it all at once. Start with one or two products or service lines, and implement changes where they can be profitable. Do not lose sight of the profit. After all, that's what sustainability is all about. If a business isn't making a profit, it will fail. Then we all lose the opportunity to work for or be served by a green business. You must balance environmental, social, and economic considerations. The companies that crack this green product nut will be the new financial winners and social heroes in the green business revolution.

Chapter 10

Greening the Package—
We Can Do Better

You know the frustration. It's the holidays and you are helping a child open her gifts. It takes longer to break into the blister pack or box than it ever did to make the product. Getting to the toy makes you want to scream. You may even get a few cuts or bruises from the razor sharp edges of the plastic or flaps on the box. When everything is finally open and the toys are extricated from their plastic bands that hold them to a cardboard thingy, it takes another hour to sort toys from the plastic, plastic from cardboard, and to break down the boxes for recycling. The child loves the gift, but the overpackaging drives you crazy and makes you wonder why you ever bought it in the first place.

Most consumers would love to see packaging go away, but that isn't a practical solution. Consumers and product manufacturers both depend on packaging. It protects products on their journey from wherever they were made. It can also extend shelf life, keeping food, flowers, and other perishables fresh for a longer period of time. Good packaging prevents tampering. During the Tylenol crisis in 1982 seven people in the Chicago area died because someone slipped cyanide into Extra Strength Tylenol capsules while the bottles were on the store shelves. We also depend on packaging for branding and ingredient checking. So we can't do away with it, but we can improve it.

According to the EPA, packaging makes up as much as one-third of the nonindustrial solid waste stream in most parts of the developed world. At least twenty-eight countries including Britain, Germany, and Denmark, currently have laws that encourage less packaging and more recycling. Many of the European countries require product makers to take back packaging or pay for recycling it, called extended producer responsibility (EPR). Typically with required takebacks, manufacturers don't actually take back their package but pay an organization to guarantee its recovery. In the U.S. there is a national law for recycling rechargeable batteries. Container deposits are also considered a form of EPR. In the

U.S., ten states have mandatory deposits on beer and soft drink containers – two states expanded this to other drinks but there are no mandates beyond containers and batteries. There is, however, much concern about package waste in both state and local governments so things will no doubt be changing soon.

Beyond the obvious waste issues there are other environmental challenges with packaging that need to be addressed by business. Plastic film and hard plastic packaging is made from petroleum, which is expensive and not a renewable resource. Some packaging is made from toxic materials such as polyvinyl chloride (PVC) and polycarbonate. Add to those issues the problem that a large amount of packaging cannot be readily recycled, including many plastics. Moreover, the current methods of packaging can add to the weight of a product, requiring more energy to move it and resulting in more greenhouse gases.

E-commerce is causing a packaging crisis of its own. Products ordered from Internet-based stores result in massive amounts of individual packaging, including corrugated paperboard and plastic. If a consumer went to a retail store instead, she would take the CD, DVD, or book home in a bag, not in a box containing void fill material. Most retailers have some kind of packaging recovery infrastructure, but most homes don't. In 2000, corrugated and plastic packaging represented about 25 percent of all discarded packaging.

All of these issues are the reason that sustainable packaging is the buzz in the packaging industry and in companies pursuing green. Sustainable packaging is packaging that is benign: it doesn't pollute, use up resources, or harm the environment. That's a tall order to fill. Just as no product is perfectly green today, no packaging wins perfect marks for sustainability. But heading in this direction has many advantages for a business that is willing to try. As with other green strategies, any small change you make can potentially save you money and limit the damage to the planet.

The bottom-line benefits for businesses include lighter weight and smaller products, reducing transportation costs, materials, energy, and greenhouse gas releases.

Many retailers are developing their own standards for greener packaging. Some will only do business with suppliers that practice sustainable packaging, which meets certain environmental criteria. You may be forced to green your packaging in order to get it on the shelves.

How do you meet the sustainable packaging challenge? Until there are uniform requirements, it will be confusing. Packaging is rapidly changing as retailers, manufacturers, and governments work through the possibilities. But there is still much you can do. Use the Seven Rs of Sustainable Packaging to help you understand the principles and guide your business in developing a green packaging strategy that fits your needs.

> Reduce packaging by minimizing the materials when designing packaging. Packaging design can be an integral part of what makes your product green.

> Remove excess by eliminating redundant packaging. It's easy to get caught up in doing things the same way that you have always done them. Ask why, and keep asking it until you are convinced that you've found the right solution.

> Reuse materials. Find a way to set aside used materials and reuse them for packaging so that discarding materials is the last resort.

> Recycle materials that can be recycled. Don't discard them. Incorporate the highest content of postconsumer recycled material that you can find into your packaging.

> Renewable materials should be chosen for packaging. Plant-based materials are almost always preferable to petroleum-based materials. If you must use petroleum materials, use the smallest amount possible.

> Revenue neutrality is key. Keep the packaging cost the same or less when all factors including transportation are taken into account. Like all things that aim to be sustainable, your packaging decisions must balance between the environmental, social, and economic good.

> Read as much as you can find on the subject of sustainable packaging. Educate your business about the latest green packaging technologies and implement those ideas that make sense for your operation.

The Sustainable Packaging Coalition, a project of GreenBlue (*www.greenblue.org*), takes these principles even further with criteria that include not only environmental principles, but also more broadly defined sustainability objectives. Safety and health for individuals and communities are additional objectives that are included in their overall criteria, along with the idea of cradle-to-cradle life cycles that were explored in the last chapter. Their approach blends business consideration of costs with a life cycle approach. They have come up with the Cadillac of green packaging principles.

The Sustainable Packaging Coalition's principles for packaging include:

> It is beneficial, safe, and healthy for individuals and communities throughout its life cycle.

> It meets market criteria for performance and cost.

> It is sourced, manufactured, transported, and recycled using renewable energy.

> It maximizes the use of renewable or recycled sources.

> It is manufactured using clean production technologies and best practices.

> It is made from materials healthy in all probable end-of-life scenarios.

> It is physically designed to optimize materials and energy.

> It is effectively recovered and used in biological and/or indus-
  trial cradle-to-cradle cycles.

If these concepts are new to you or your organization, they may seem a bit overwhelming. This chapter will help you better understand green packaging by giving you information about new, greener materials and by further explaining techniques that reduce packaging materials.

Opportunity: Less Is More

Not only can packaging be irritating, it can also be illegal. In 2007, San Francisco banned plastic bags at supermarkets. In 2008 China, in an effort to return to reusable cloth bags and baskets, banned free plastic bags common at many retailers and ordered that custom-ers be charged for their use. Several U.S. cities have, or are trying, to ban the sale of bottled water in their city offices to discourage plastic waste. Chicago is heavily taxing bottled water. Packaging, in particular plastic packaging, is on the brink of becoming an environmental and moral stigma.

Bagging Green

Plastic bags are cheap to produce and lightweight, which is the reason that they have been so widely used for many years. According to the Film and Bag Federation, 100 billion plastic bags are used worldwide each year. The problem with plastic bags or packaging is that they are rarely recycled. What's more, once they are thrown away no one really knows how long it will take for plastic to degrade in a landfill. Some say that a plastic bag will take 1,000 years to biodegrade. Other scientists say that it won't ever breakdown completely but instead will break into smaller toxic plastic beads that will find their way into our food chain. A Canadian teenager recently isolated plastic-eating bacteria, but until industry capitalizes on this, we must reduce our use of plastic.

Reducing plastic packaging—or any packaging for that matter—is not easy. For grocery stores and other retail outlets, it means retraining or educating customers to bring something with them that is reusable. In France, shoppers carry durable, woven market baskets. Produce, dairy, meats, and household items all go in the basket. U.S. food retailers are in the process of retraining customers to use cloth bags, but it isn't happening overnight.

What ever happened to the idea of reusable packaging? In the old days milk bottles were returned to the milkman for reuse. Certain applications like liquid containers could be designed for reuse today. Typically, it is more sustainable to reuse than recycle. If you decide to look into reuse for your business's packaging, be sure to design the package for durability. Also, make sure preparing the container for reuse does not expend too many resources. A glass bottle that is collected from the consumer, sterilized, and transported to a manufacturer to refill requires a certain amount of energy for that journey. If you are considering this option, make sure that the energy and resources used in this journey don't exceed recycling and repurposing of the glass.

There are some good examples of applying the principle that "less is more" to packaging. IKEA has turned packaging into an art and reduced transportation costs by 15 percent per item through its "flat packaging" design. Their unique packaging design has made each box as small as possible to perfectly fit their goods leaving barely a spare millimeter. Not only does this mean that they can get more in a truck when products are shipped, but there is also a smaller box for consumers to deal with when they unpack their products. By implementing careful product design that simultaneously considers the packaging, they reduce their costs for transportation and materials.

Less is also more when it comes to packaging at Intel, where the Logistics Transport Materials Engineering Team is dedicated to designing packaging that saves natural resources and money. They have redesigned the packaging used to ship CPUs so that more products can fit in a shipping box. They also eliminated the plastic foam cushioning and replaced it with more sustainable paper cushioning. Intel is a mammoth corporation, which may allow them to devote an entire team of professionals to this kind of project. Smaller businesses should watch what the big companies are doing. See if you can use any of the technology or best practices in your operation.

If your company has not looked at its strategies for packaging for a few years, it's time. There have been advances in sustainable materials and money-saving techniques. If you are filling voids in boxes, stop using foam peanuts. Consumers hate them, and they are usually made from not-so-earth-friendly foam. Newer paper fill products can be recycled. Consider using air pillow systems, which are versatile and light. True, the air pillow systems are made from a thin plastic shell, but the amount of plastic used is small compared to other materials. An air bubble fills most of the void. The consumer can then pop the plastic air bubble and compress the plastic, eventually recycling it along with other plastic bags.

Secondary packaging is another area in which businesses can improve their packaging. Secondary packaging includes plastic wrap that keeps boxes of goods safely on pallets between warehouse and retail outlets. This kind of packaging is used extensively and mostly ends up in landfills. There may not yet be a better alternative for holding goods in place during shipping, but it is worthwhile to take a close look at the wrapping process with the plastic film. Certainly you can train your workers to at least reduce the amount of plastic used.

Opportunity: New Materials

Reduced packaging isn't always possible. Some products need a lot of protection during shipping or have other packaging requirements that cannot easily be redesigned. Food products, for example, need protection to prolong their shelf life or are required by law to have certain packaging. Fortunately green chemistry is coming to the rescue with packaging technologies that are currently in their infancy but will soon be mainstream.

In the 1967 movie, *The Graduate*, Ben Braddock's neighbor whispered a hot employment tip in his ear: "Plastics." And the tip was right. (Decades earlier, in *It's a Wonderful Life*, Sam Wainwright, George Bailey's childhood friend, made all his millions in plastics during World War II and gave George much the same advice. George ignored him and ended up, on the whole, a happier man for it.) The petroleum plastics industry has grown enormously since 1967, and plastics can be found in everything today from furniture to cars. It is also one of the main materials used in packaging. This use of petroleum-based plastic will most likely decrease as greenhouse gas production, environmental health awareness, and the rising cost of oil inspire new technologies. Several companies around the world have created plastic packaging out of new, greener material called bioplastics.

Bioplastics are currently primarily made from field corn. The corn is harvested and broken down into corn sugar. The corn sugar, or dextrose, is turned into lactic acid through fermentation and a distilling process. The lactic acid is then transformed into pellets of bioplastic, which can be turned into packaging or containers. The benefits of this type of plastic over petroleum-based plastics are many. Corn is a renewable resource, while petroleum is nonrenewable. The resins are also produced at a lower temperature, saving energy and greenhouse gasses. There are no known toxic additives to bioplastics. In fact, some companies make hypoallergenic pillows and other nonallergenic products from corn plastics. Another benefit is that packaging made from bioplastic is biodegradable.

Although bioplastics seem like the perfect solution to the packaging problem, there are still some kinks to be worked out. Yes, packaging and products made from bioplastics are biodegradable, but only under the right conditions. There has been pushback by environmentalists, because the conditions for biodegradability are specific and, as of yet, are sometimes hard to fulfill. Some bioplastics can degrade in a backyard compost heap within a few months, but most need the higher temperature and humidity of an industrial composting facility. Consumers, the end user of this type of packaging, typically don't realize that the packaging needs special treatment, so they're confused about whether to throw it in the garbage or put it in the recycle bin. The reality is that in most cities, most bioplastic packaging is still ending up in traditional waste disposal sites where it can't biodegrade.

Another unresolved environmental issue with bioplastics is that currently they are made from corn, as is bioethanol that we use in our cars. This has raised the price of corn, perhaps making the cost savings not as appealing as once thought. Environmentalists say that the environmental footprint of corn is too large to be a truly green alternative. Currently, corn cultivation requires a large amount of resources, including water, fertilizer, and energy to plant, harvest, and transport it. When all the inputs, emissions, and pollution from runoff are taken into account, corn is arguably not much greener than petroleum.

The bioplastic industry is in its infancy, and these issues will hopefully be worked out in the near future. It is a transitional solution while we continue to look for the best eco-packaging. It is likely, however, that cities and waste haulers will figure out how to tell consumers what must be done to biodegrade or recycle bioplastics. As for the corn debate, innovations in green chemistry will make it possible—hopefully in the not-too-distant future—to distill bioplastics from other feedstocks like switch grass or the leftover stocks from agriculture. In fact, there are already some innovations in the works. A California company, Cereplast, is manufacturing hybrid resins that are replacing 50 percent or more of the petroleum content in traditional plastic products, using materials from renewable sources such as corn, tapioca, wheat, and potatoes.

Another interesting trend in sustainable packaging of smaller consumer goods is the plantable box. Once the consumer has opened the box, he gets rid of the container by going into the yard, digging a hole, and planting it. The box is biodegradable and compostable. Some brands, such as Pangea, infuse the packaging with seeds so that once in the ground it gives birth to plants. This is the ultimate cradle-to-cradle concept in packaging. It may not work for large boxes—say, those large enough to fit a computer or television—but for small consumer products, it's a clever green idea that returns the packaging materials to nature.

Of course, one of the most common green packaging strategies any company can implement is to purchase packaging material made from recycled content. This can include paperboard, corrugated cartons, molded paper, or plastics. It is possible to source 100 percent recycled paper packaging options, also known as molded pulp packaging. It can be cost effective and a greener choice compared with other packaging solutions because it is made with recycled paper that can quickly biodegrade. If molded paper is not an option for your packaging application, you can still press for recycled content materials. First, find out from your supplier the percentage of recycled content in the material. Then, find out if it includes postconsumer recycled content and, if so, the percentage. Be aware that some manufacturers combine postconsumer and preconsumer recycled content, blurring the environmental benefit.

Sustainable packaging materials are still in the early stages of development, but it is well worth the effort to learn more about what is available for your particular needs. Partnering with a packaging company that is involved in one of these green innovations is a good way to get started with a greener packaging strategy.

Opportunity: Labeling

When you make decisions about what kind of packaging to use and how to size it, find a balance between proper branding and sustainability. Many food products, for example, need to convey a certain amount of information to the consumer, and the packaging is an important vehicle for that information. The day may be coming when shoppers can use a gizmo the size of a cell phone while they walk through any store to scan any product and pull up any information about that product. In concept, the information will include such things as corporate social responsibility of a company, where the product was made, any warnings, and its environmental footprint. Once this becomes possible, brands will get by with less packaging, because they won't need to convey much of an overt message.

Until that day, there are some green labeling practices that businesses should consider. Today, green product labels are confusing—for the business and even more so for the consumer. There are many competing and one-attribute green consumer labels competing for space and attention. Originally, there were recycling codes for various types of plastics and a recycling symbol, the circular arrows or Mobius loop, denoting that the product is recyclable. As green has become more popular but without universally accepted standards, all kinds of newer symbols and logos have begun to show up on packages. The problem is that only a relatively small group of consumers know what they mean. Consumers who don't know what they mean ignore most of these new symbols.

The Carbon Trust has a carbon label. The European Union has the Eco-label. Canada has the Environmental Choice label. Many other countries have their own label with their own set of standards. In the United States we have Energy Star, Green Seal, Scientific Certification Systems, Sustainable Forestry Initiative, Forest Stewardship Council, Fair Trade, and Energy Guide. Then, there is

WRAP for the apparel industry, UTZ for coffee and other agriculture products, LEED for green buildings, and Certified Organic label for food and cotton. And these are just the "green" labels; there are other labels for other attributes of various products too, like nutrition labels for food, care labels for clothing, or warning labels for chemical products. It has become a labeling morass, with no end in sight to the confusion and proliferation of more labels. Packaging will need to grow just to accommodate the labels espousing the products' greenness and other attributes.

The solution, of course, is to align your company and products with the standards and labels that are the most meaningful to your customer. At some point in the future, standards will be global, rather than segmented by country and product type. Meanwhile, the solution is to choose labels judiciously. Use minimally sized labels, consistent with your product packing, with high postconsumer content and soy inks. Then, add quick-dissolving, less-toxic adhesives, and you've created a recipe for greener labels. If nothing else, avoid labels that are confusing or meaningless to your customer.

Easy Steps to Green

Sustainable packaging is a rapidly growing practice that is here to stay. The concept needs to be further developed and standardized, and that will happen in the not-too-distant future. Greening your packaging and label is a key way for your business to further prove its commitment to the environment and sustainability even if the actual product has not yet been greened. Learn as much as you can, and begin implementing small changes in your company's packaging. This will help ensure that your company keeps pace with expectations from the marketplace. These four tips will help you get started with some useful green packaging strategies.

1. Talk to Your Current Supplier

Ask if he knows about sustainable packaging and has any options for you. If he does, open the dialogue for possible strategies and the associated costs. If he doesn't, see if he would be willing to explore this with you and figure out something that is more sustainable for your product. You can learn together, and he might be willing to do the groundwork and research at his own cost. Or, at the very least, he may be willing to share the cost of hiring a consultant or designer for the new packaging concept.

2. Develop Metrics for Progress

It is critical to measure various benchmarks related to packaging. You can start by stating an overall goal: for example, reducing packaging by 5–10 percent or reducing the carbon footprint of your packaging by 20 percent over the next three years. Goals must be doable, measurable, and have a timeline. Then, break the bigger goal into strategies. For instance, plan to reduce the size of the packaging by X percent or increase the content of postconsumer recycled material in your packaging by X percent. Once you have the strategies, you are ready to go to vendors for help in achieving them. If you are a large enough manufacturer, it would be wise to form a stakeholder group, including your packaging vendor, to develop your goals and metrics. Coming up with goals and standards for your packaging will give you an edge over your competitors.

3. Continuous Improvement

Once you have metrics and have started to improve your packaging, don't rest on your laurels. Continue to make your packaging more sustainable. If you are starting with cardboard that is 30 percent postconsumer recycled material, push for 40 percent within a reasonable timeframe. If some of your packaging is already made with a bioplastic, start educating yourself about bioplastic sources that are not corn based. Every six months ask vendors and suppliers what they can do to help you make your packaging more sustainable.

4. Stay Informed

Join a group such as the Sustainable Packaging Coalition to keep up on the latest in best practices and technological advances for green packaging materials. Or participate in a packaging trade organization that has a sustainable packaging committee. There are plenty of conferences and forums on the subject that can be attended for a fee, even if you're not a member. Conferences are a way to get up to speed on this complicated subject very quickly, with minimal time and expense. Trade and industry publications are typically a credible source for information but will lag behind the organizations that are built specifically around sustainability.

Part III

How Do I Get Them to Care

Chapter 11

Selling Green Up and Down the Ranks—Bosses and Employees

Most organizations that start doing some random green initiatives rely on their community affairs liaison or the marketing department to tell the outside world the company is going green. But like all real lasting personal or organizational change, just telling people you are doing something doesn't make it so. A real and lasting change must start in the organization itself and be manifested by its employees. If that's not the case, the attempt to green risks being shallow and temporary, failing before it even gets off the ground. True green changes in an organization need to be authentic and sustained over time.

Companies and products are being scrutinized more than ever these days based on their green claims. If a company declares itself green, it better be able to pass the sniff test and have some substantial initiatives in the works. Consumers are aware of and intolerant of disingenuous corporate behavior. The blogosphere is full of skeptics, alerting consumers 24/7 to bogus or hyped up green claims. To ensure success and lasting change, make sure that green is ubiquitous in your organization.

Before you make sure that green is in all your company does, you must first make sure your employees and colleagues are aware of it. This can happen in as many different ways as there are organizations.

In my company, for example, green started to percolate because, as the owner and CEO, I began to talk about it, ask questions, and demand that sustainability become part of the company's genetic makeup. The green ethic came from the top and filtered down through the ranks.

Sometimes, the pressure to go green comes from outside the company. If companies are doing it, we sometimes assume consumers must have been asking for it. That happens in some cases, but often when it comes to greening an organization, the transformation starts in the company first. Often one person or a small group of employees spearheads the green effort. In some companies, the

CEO is persuaded by fellow industry CEOs to make a green commitment, such as becoming carbon neutral. The CEO may not even know what the commitment to be carbon neutral means, but he or she signs a pledge because others in the industry are doing it.

Other companies are pressured by their supply chain. Maybe their biggest customers ask them to green their packaging. Still other companies have a small group of well-intentioned employees who get together and discuss how their company could be greener, trying to figure out how to get agreement from higher-ups. In some organizations, the corporate board of directors has already made a commitment to CSR and have corporate social responsibility reporting requirements that become the green impetus, keeping their company on track to being more environmentally correct.

Green Interns

Some green business initiatives have started unexpectedly with a summer intern or entry-level employee who was involved in campus ecology at her university. She begins working in a company and is shocked that the most basic environmental practices, like recycling or turning out lights, are ignored. She starts talking about it and getting other people interested. Suddenly, a green initiative has begun in a place that never thought of it before because a new set of eyes looks differently on the same four walls and same old way of doing things, creating new green possibilities.

The reality is that greening a business doesn't just happen on its own. As with other changes in an organization, someone within the organization must see that a change is needed. A champion, or better yet, champions, must lead the change. And the organization must have the time, energy, and the political will to make it through the transition period. The larger the organization, the more time, effort, and political will it will take to make the shift. This is good news for smaller organizations; greening can often be done on a shoestring budget.

No matter what the size of the organization, to be successful a shift to green must permeate the entire company. In short, the corporate leadership must make as much of an effort to sell green inside the organization as they do to sell it to the world outside. What will make people in your organization from the top-level management to the summer intern understand the need to go green? This chapter will help you get it on everyone's radar screen and keep it there for the long-term green journey, helping your business to become authentically green.

Green Motivation

There have been many theories about how to get people to adopt earth-friendly behaviors.

> The moral theory. People want to do what is right, like choose not to throw trash out the car window. Appeal to their better instincts, and they'll follow you.

> The economic theory. People are motivated to do something if it benefits their pocket book. For example, when gasoline reaches a high enough price, the majority of people will buy fuel-efficient cars.

> The scare 'em to death theory. People will adopt new behaviors if they fear that not doing so will have negative consequences for themselves or those they love. That kind of psychology was unsuccessfully used for years to try to convince people to stop smoking.

A recent theory, based on a study by a psychologist at Arizona State University, Robert Cialdini, implies that people will adopt green behaviors because their friends and neighbors have already adopted them—a herd mentality theory. Cialdini's theory is based on the belief that human beings have an instinctual desire to be part of a group and follow the pack. People don't want to be left out; there is safety in numbers.

Cialdini further argues that people are more likely to follow the largest group of informed individuals, not one renegade leader. You are more likely to go to a new restaurant if some friends whom you trust rave about it. You are also more likely to put out your recycling if several of your neighbors already do it. If your neighbors or peer group own fuel-efficient cars, you will probably buy one too. It is the same mentality that has us all trying to keep up with the Jones's.

You can apply this methodology to greening an organization. To do it effectively, you need to get the attention of the herd—everyone in the organization—and then get them all going in the same green direction. To do this you also need to get the leaders, whether actual leaders or perceived leaders, to go there first.

Selling Green Up the Ranks

You are reading this book, so you are clearly interested in helping your organization become greener. But you can't do it alone. It doesn't matter if you are part of the leadership group or not; you will still need to convince the leadership that this idea is worth pursuing. When you are considering whom you need to reach, remember that leaders are often managers, but managers aren't always leaders. In other words, make sure that you get those whom others look up to in your organization to implement a green strategy.

Often the best way to reach superiors in your organization is to help them understand that they are not the first to have a green initiative. Many do not want to be the first to try something, because it may fail. If other groups, preferably from the same industry, have had a good result with trying something new, others will also try it.

On the other hand, most organizations don't want to be the last to do something new either. If leaders are the last to adopt something, they may face ridicule from their peers or lose customers and profits to those who adopted the practice earlier. Most organizations, like most people, want to be in the center of the herd.

To convince leaders they are neither the first nor the last, you must make a realistic presentation of facts and figures. Collecting information about green initiatives for any industry is fairly easy. Start by doing Internet searches using your industry name, plus the terms, *sustainable, green, environmentally responsible,* or *carbon footprint.* Another good resource is your industry professional or trade organizations. Many have probably explored the possibility of forming an industry green group to begin to address environmental issues. Gather information about what other similar organizations are doing to go green. This will help take away the fear of the unknown for your company leaders.

Use the general green market information in the first section of this book. Build the case that greening is already being done and that the market has begun to accept the change. Make sure to point out some of the benefits greening can bring, such as cost savings, competitive advantage, and a smaller carbon footprint.

Sometimes it's not possible to reach the entire leadership of the organization. In that case, find one accessible person in the leadership whom you think is open to the possibility of greening the organization. Strike up a casual conversation about something you are doing in your home that has increased energy efficiency. Maybe you can approach someone in management who drives a fuel-efficient car. He might be a green ally. Find some green common ground and use the conversation to gauge if he would be open to discussing an initiative within the company. Starting this conversation may actually be easier than you think given the cost of gasoline these days. Everyone seems to be interested in energy savings, even if they don't have a clue about green business.

Selling Green Sideways

Green is quickly becoming mainstream, so rest assured there are people in your organization who share your desire to save the planet. Start by trying to find some colleagues on the greener end of the behavior spectrum (review Chapter 2 in the first section of the book). You'll probably know these people already. They may walk, bicycle, carpool, or take a bus to work rather than drive an SUV. They may brag about their locally grown produce and their organic bag lunches. They may shop at a food co-op or talk about their summer family backpacking vacations. Find them and form a casual green employee group. A green group, even if it is not a workplace-sanctioned program, can have a big impact within the organization. There is power in numbers. These groups are often more successful at getting green on the radar screen than individual efforts.

How Green Was My Company

Even as the owner of my own company, I have had challenges in going green. I had my own personal green epiphany, but my management team had not. They did not come to the same Business for Social Responsibility meetings. They didn't hear the success stories that I had heard. They did not experience the excitement in the company owners' voices when they told how they were trying to grow organic grapes at their winery or hunt for natural ingredients for soaps and lotions in South America. Therefore, my management team did not initially understand why I would want to change the way we were doing things. I had to spend the time and effort to get them as excited about this green change as I was. At the time, it seemed overwhelming to try to do this on my own.

My strategy was to assemble a group of consultants who could help us figure out what going green meant in the property management industry. Then they helped us put together a plan for how we could accomplish greening.

> Having experts on my side gave me more credibility and helped convince and inspire my team. Once the management team was jazzed and we figured out the scope of our initiative, we worked on the next step: selling it to the employees.

Today it is less challenging to find a team to persuade the top brass to go green. Most industries have at least a few companies that have successful greening initiatives underway. In fact, companies specializing in greening facilities have formed their own widely accepted industry. It is easy to find engineers, architects, and suppliers in any area of the country who have green building experience. Use these established consultants and practices to help bring your company peers along. This is an important step so that they are willing to commit the time and energy to take on a new initiative. It will be one more thing that they will need to be responsible for in an already jam-packed day. They need to be excited about greening and understand it, because they will ultimately be responsible for sending that same excitement through the ranks of the employees.

Selling Down the Ranks

Selling green down the ranks can be trickier than selling up or sideways. Don't take short cuts. It is absolutely critical to get agreement from rank-and-file employees in order to make any organizational greening a sustained success. I learned this lesson the hard way. In hindsight, it was much easier to get my management team to go along with my green ideas than to get the employees up to speed, sustain that level of knowledge, and then maintain the enthusiasm to keep it going.

At first, we set up regular green meetings for employees every other week for the first six months to educate them about all of the different facets of greening our property management practices. At each meeting we learned together about a practice that we could use to green our properties. We had vendors come in and talk about their environmentally sensitive products or services, like organic lawn care or integrated pest management techniques. At other meetings we asked government agency reps from the pollution control agency to talk about recycling alternatives or healthy water issues. We also had speakers from health and environmental nonprofits, like the American Lung Association, to talk about the health effects of cleaning chemicals and paints. Our employees got a crash course in green and found access to vendors ready and willing to help green our properties.

Problems started when we didn't keep our education of green practices going. We occasionally still had vendors come in over the next few years, but because of employee turnover we needed to start over with the green education for each new hire. We didn't continue the intensive training that we had at the beginning of the initiative. Instead, we developed a manual for greening our properties, containing information about each green component of our initiative together with a list of vendors. We gave the manual to each new hire to read and use. Without spending the time and effort that we had in the beginning, our green initiative began to lose its way.

Between employee turnover, no eco-education, and a shift to a different type of property that we managed, we floundered. Our green program dwindled to a few articles in our newsletter and some green building initiatives in our own office space. It took a number of years to realize the problem. We had stopped energizing and educating the employees about the importance of being green at work. Even though two leaders in my company had deep-seated green values, we failed to infuse it into the company as it grew and changed by not bringing the employees along. The good news is that I did learn a thing or two from this experience.

To implement a successful green program, employees must have a team mindset.

It is essential to bring employees along at every stage of greening, keeping the enthusiasm high. Change only truly happens when it becomes personal. This occurs when employees begin to translate their learned green behavior from work to other parts of their life. Once green permeates both their personal and work life, change can be sustained.

Greening employees can be accomplished with employee groups that are formed to discuss green practices at work as well as at home. We called them eco-teams, but they can be labeled anything. Employees get points for bringing ideas to work that help the greening efforts and also for bringing ideas for greening from work to home. Teams keep track of their points. Every six months the team with the most points gets a prize, such as a lunch at a restaurant or tickets to a play or ball game.

Another way to get the team green mentality going is to have a contest around good green lifestyle changes, such as commuting. Employees get points on a publicly displayed chart for using less energy to get around. Each desired green activity—for example, biking to work or carpooling—is assigned a number of points. The more you want to encourage the activity, the more points you can attribute to the activity. For example, employees may get five points for biking or walking to work and four points for taking the bus or train. If they take the stairway instead of the elevator they get one point. At the end of the month, the points are totaled, and people win based on their number of points. It is a good way to keep it continuously on employees' minds. It really works. People engage in the contest and change their behavior as they see others on the chart doing it.

Selling Green to Your Supply Chain

If you outsource or subcontract any work and expect it to mesh with your green philosophy, you will need to provide your subcontractors green codes of conduct to follow. Even though they are not employees of your business, they are an extension of your organization, and their behavior will reflect on your company. You have given an implied approval to the way they operate by hiring and paying them. Be diligent about giving them your expectations of social responsibility, not only about the end result of the job or the product, but about how you want the job done or the product created. This is green business 101, and it is critical.

Before the global economy kicked into high gear, it was common practice to hire a subcontractor and allow him to figure out how to produce the product, how to treat his employees, and where to get his materials. The only concern for your organization was how to get the best price and service from the subcontractor. But now that so many things are outsourced in far-flung countries with laws, values, and cultures vastly different from our own, it's necessary to spell out expectations with codes of conduct. Since a high-profile, alleged sweatshop labor incident in the mid-1990s, the retail industry has developed labor-related codes of conduct for subcontractors and vendors. Today, with green products starting to be big business, environmental or sustainability codes will be the next generation of conduct codes we'll request from subcontractors.

This will most likely begin with the large retail companies. But all organizations, no matter the size or industry, could benefit from giving subcontractors clear green direction. Sustainability codes should dovetail with a business's green product or service standards discussed in the Chapter 9. In my property management firm, we are currently developing sustainability codes for our vendors that service our properties. The codes will include requirements that vendors provide a green alternative to their standard product or service. For example, a lawn contractor must be able to provide organic lawn care as an alternative to a chemical weed-and-feed program. Only vendors and subcontractors that meet our standards will get the job, and the sustainability codes will be a binding part of our contracts.

Abiding by a sustainability code allows subcontractors to learn about green. Granted, it may be forced learning, but if they want the business, they will do it. They can always reject the relationship if they wish. Also, the sustainability code will clearly communicate your green expectations. As your policies become green, it is important to have such clear communication. Finally, it gives you some assurance that the work will be done consistent with your organization's value system and image.

The other pieces of this green supply chain puzzle are inspections and third-party audits. It may not be enough to communicate sustainability codes and assume that they are being followed. The next level of green in the outsourcing world is to arrange surprise onsite visits or audits. This is most effectively done through a third-party auditor. Then you can be confident that your standards are followed.

A Word about Resistance

If at first you don't succeed in convincing those who are up, down, or sideways from you, or who are your supply chain, don't be discouraged. The green market is diverse and growing quickly, and you don't know what or when someone will tip from brown to green. A boss or employee who is currently uninterested in greening the organization may change her mind within a few months time because of something she read in the media or saw on television. Or perhaps her place of worship has a new emphasis on being earth friendly. Sometimes children get their parents interested. And sometimes it is pure economics, like rising fuel prices.

Green is coming at people from every direction, so it is hard to say what will persuade people to see through green lenses. Keep nudging, pushing, and suggesting. Work on getting more support from others for your green idea. Go back at a different time in the fiscal year, with a slightly different message, or find someone else in the organization who will listen.

Perseverance *does* pay off. An acquaintance of mine who works at a large multinational tried for a decade or more to get green on the company's radar screen without success. There never was any time or money for his ideas about making the company more sustainable. Then one day a new CEO was hired, and everything this manager wanted to do in the company around sustainability suddenly was not only possible but also supported with staff and money. A much larger initiative than he had ever imagined started to take form and substance. Persistence and patience are virtues when selling green inside an organization.

Vision–Mission–Values

There are people in organizations who are planners, and there are people who are doers. The planners frustrate the doers, because there is never enough planning before the doing. And of course, the doers drive the planners crazy because they want to launch into tactics without carefully mapping out the issue. Where green initiatives are in the works, it pays to plan and go back to basics. Everyone in an organization needs to be on the same page in order for a green initiative to be successful. To be lasting, green must permeate the heart and soul of an organization. The best way to achieve this is to make green the nucleus in your company's vision statement. If sustainability is not part of the current vision, then you must update the vision statement.

The most effective way to do this in smaller organizations is to get the ranks together and have a facilitated discussion, involving as many people as you can. This can also work well in a department setting or committee of a larger organization. Find a facilitator, and as a group imagine a vision for the organization that includes environmental responsibility. A vision statement should succinctly describe how the organization or initiative will look several years out. It describes what success looks like in five years. As an illustration, the vision for my management firm was, "We are a nationally known residential property management firm that has set the standard for sustainability in our industry."

Once the vision statement is clear, a mission statement can be easily crafted. A mission statement is the nontactical statement of how the vision will be achieved. For example, my property management firm's mission stated, "We will lead a nationwide effort to make buildings cleaner, healthier, and safer through the development and use of environmentally responsible building management standards and techniques." This mission statement has been in use for almost two decades and still applies to a larger, much-changed organization today.

Many organizations skip developing a statement of values. This is a mistake. A statement of values is the foundation for the vision and mission. It is the glue that holds everything else together. The statement of values should accurately reflect the values of the leadership of your organization. The values need to be authentic; if they are not true values that are accepted and practiced, they will not hold up to scrutiny within the organization. Some companies publish their statement of values so that they can convey more information than a short vision or mission can relate. The statement of values becomes the behavior and decision filter for the organization.

At meetings of my management firm, we often read our statement of values aloud to ground us and remind us of what we are committed to. We have five key values in this company that are sacred: partnership, innovation, personal and professional balance, sustainability, and personal and professional growth. We define the sustainability value as, "We commit to conducting our business activities in a healthy manner in order to improve and protect the health of all people, our clients, our business, and planet." The full statement with an explanation statement is on our website and in our marketing literature (*www.citiesmanagement.com*). We hold ourselves and staff strictly to all five values. We have chosen employees and clients based on these values. If you go through the effort to create a statement of values, you must use it regularly. In my company, the words have been installed permanently (and artistically) on several strategic walls of the main office where employees see it every day.

Train—Inspire, Train—Inspire, Train—Inspire

Training and inspiring is a continuous effort. It is the same when it comes to greening your organization. You must perpetually enthuse, promote, and teach sustainability within the organization. Male or female, you will be one part cheerleader, one part mentor, and two parts student of green. Things are changing so quickly with green technology, practices, and products that you will need to immerse your staff and yourself in the topic.

Easy Steps to Green

Following are five helpful tips to get you started selling green up and down the ranks of your workplace. Even though the task of convincing others is somewhat political, keep it light and in perspective, as others may be in a different place on the green behavior spectrum than you are. No tears or fears, getting the key people in your organization to move in this direction can lead to a more successful business model and a better world.

1. Tailor the Approach to the People

Years ago, a mentor told me, "Don't ever confuse a clear view for a short distance." It has been good advice on my green journey. Just because I could see the positive end result from going green, doesn't mean that others can. Many people need numbers to be convinced, some need an emotional plea. Just as I used several approaches to appeal to the mindset of various readers' perpectives in the first chapter: financial, people, environmental and touchy-feely personal. You too will need to find the best approach for the people you are trying to convince. It is not a one size fits all for everyone in the organization. Your language and tactics needs to fit your audience.

2. Provide a Plan

All business managers and owners deal daily with competing agendas and needs. One more thing to deal with, such as greening the organization, may be perceived as a burden rather than a fix. No matter your position within the organization, you can help sort through the competing interests by offering a plan of how and where to get started. Use this book as a guide and go to the management team or your employees with a plan that makes sense for your organization.

3. Don't Shame

It can be tempting to vilify those in your organization who don't understand that going green is a win-win but don't do it. It is not a "them against us" proposition. Most everyone can be brought along eventually but some people are slower when it comes to change of any kind. Keep communicating the positives and never ever shame or vilify someone who isn't there yet. People will self-select out if they become too uncomfortable by your greening and will be replaced by others who embrace it. On the other hand, vendors that can't live up to your requests for green can often be easily replaced by those that can.

4. Find a Support Group

If you have little or no support for greening within the organization, go outside for it. Support may be as close as a nonprofit organization with an environmental mission in your industry. Or you may find a vendor with a green mission that supplies or could supply a critical function to your business. The vendor could help you convince management or employees. Search out a partner in green and brainstorm approaches to use inside your organization.

5. Model Green Fun

Most people are suckers for fun. If you can make green fun rather than a burden, you will convince the skeptics more quickly. As hokey as it might be, run contests, start teams and give away prizes for good green behavior.

Understand as you put your time and energy into sustainability that you will never be the same. You will learn things in the process of greening your organization that you will use at home. You will also try things at home that you can bring to your business. All of it will be useful to you, whether you own the business or are a rising star in your organization. All that you learn and all that you know will help to protect and enrich you, your organization, your industry, and the planet.

Chapter 12

Marketing Green— a Formula for Success

At some point it will be time for you to tell the outside world that the greening process is underway within your organization. Ideally, it is after the organization is confident that it has enough green woven throughout its fabric to introduce it into marketing efforts. Knowing if an organization is green enough to tell anyone on the outside is very subjective. There is no magical formula for green enough. Single-attribute greening (greening only one thing in the organization) typically isn't green enough. For instance, if you make housewares and begin to introduce bamboo as a sustainable material into one line of products but your company building is irresponsibly burning through other resources, it is risky to publicize yourself as a green company. Yes, it is a good start to integrate greener materials into design, but remember that green implies a holistic approach. Many companies have been taken to task for this kind of one-attribute whack at being green.

An intelligent approach to green marketing is to have green initiatives started in all three key areas of facility, operations, and products or services. Of course, the ultimate in green legitimacy would be to have sustainability permeate every nook and cranny of the organization before you shout it to the world. But that can take too long, so finding a reasonable green level is a good idea. One way to decide when you've reached green enough is to check out how other organizations in your industry are talking about being green. Are they doing it well? Have they been successfully communicating? What does success look like? Have they taken any flack for it?

If no one in your industry is marketing green yet, you may be the trailblazer. Or perhaps, like me, you have been a pioneer and have been tinkering with your green initiatives and marketing for years. No matter your experience, there are some basic principles that you need to understand and heed for success in marketing. Green marketing has its risks, but on the flipside, when it is done well and honestly it is packed with rewards.

Whether you call it green marketing, green communication, or green initiative announcements, all these efforts have one goal: a movement to action. Depending on the organization's mission, that action can take many forms, such as getting consumers to buy more product, more services, or believe in a brand. In the United States, consumers have yet to be moved to frenzied, green buying action. Yes, hybrid cars are selling better since gas prices are higher, and eco-friendly soap is increasingly found in laundry rooms, but the movement to recognize green as responsible consumption has been slow compared to other parts of the world. Part of the blame may lie with lackluster marketing efforts.

The early green marketing efforts of the mid-1990s were bold and outrageous. Some European retailers cut their success out of provocative ads that linked them to various humanitarian causes in which their consumers believed. The billboard and magazine ads were controversial and grabbed viewers at a visceral level. They were very clever and appealed to a large young audience.

Since the mid-1990s, sustainability and green have become far more widely accepted, but marketing on the subject has become staid and boring. Current advertisements try to educate, but they don't have a strong call to action.

Green Marketing Benefits

If you can get the green message right, there are big benefits for your organization.

Green marketing helps sell more of whatever you are selling. The market for green continues to expand. More people are aware of earth-friendly options and are willing to purchase green.

Green marketing can differentiate you from your competition. To do this effectively, your organization must be confident about being a market leader rather than blending into the rest of the industry.

If your organization has some green initiatives in place and others in your space don't, market with a green theme to make you stand out from the crowd and give you an edge over the competition. The ultimate benefit, of course, is becoming the market leader and enjoying the largest market share for a longer period of time.

Green marketing is making sure your business doesn't lag the market. As more and more organizations go green, if your organization doesn't get with the times, your business will be behind the curve, which may result in lost market share.

Green marketing helps consumer education. Currently, consumers are educated about environmental products and services in some industries like housing and food, but there is still a long way to go. There is a surprising gap in consumer green knowledge regarding simple concepts such as recycling or energy-use reduction. There is still much confusion and a lack of understanding about green products and services. Businesses can provide needed education through their advertising and communication efforts, which will ultimately bring more sales.

Green marketing gives off the halo effect. If you are a green organization and sell a green product or service, in the eyes of your customers you are better than your competition. I experienced this often with my management firm after we started our green initiative. Clients thought that we were more trustworthy, honest, and better because we had a property management program that cared for the planet. We care for the planet; thus we will care about them because we just plain care. Although there is no way of knowing exactly how much this contributed to our success over the years, we are the market leader in our region, and I believe that we achieved this position, in part, because of the halo effect.

Greenwashing

There are pitfalls to avoid when marketing green. If you don't execute a green marketing program correctly, you can hurt your campaign or, worse, your reputation. These presumed risks may be the reason that we don't see much bold and brave green-centric advertising these days. Possibly the biggest risk to companies is being accused of greenwashing.

Greenwashing means to purposely mislead consumers about the environmental practices of an organization or the environmental benefits of the product or service your organization is marketing. Given that no service or product is perfectly green, greenwashing labels have been attached to both deserving and undeserving brands. A large part of the problem is the lack of universal standards for green. If everyone, including consumers and business, agreed about what makes a product or service green, greenwashing would recede as an issue. More on this in the next chapter, but know the risk is real.

Green initiatives, by their nature, should provide a boost to your organization's credibility. Some consumers see it as an intrinsic value added to a product or service. However, if you don't back up your green initiative by verifiable activities and real green changes, you'll lose credibility. Consumers and green watchdog groups may work to damage your organization's reputation and brand. So do it right. Don't ever engage in phony greening.

Because there is so much more green in advertising and the media than ever before, there is also the risk of green fatigue with the consumer. Since many media outlets are doing more green stories and companies are advertising more green products, audiences may at some point reach the saturation point. We are still far from a green saturation point, but you can avoid the possibility of green fatigue altogether by changing your message from time to time.

Green messaging needs to evolve just as any other marketing program changes with the times.

When marketing a product or service as green, you also run the risk that the public doesn't yet see a need for it. We ran into this when we were deciding how to market our paperless software product. The software saves a tremendous amount of paper, but the statistics showed that paper use was increasing. Our paperless pitch didn't seem to resonate with prospective clients. We made a decision in 2005 to hold off on marketing any green benefits of the product. Instead, we focused on the gained efficiency when the product was used. Recently we decided to reintroduce a green marketing program for the software because in the past twelve months green building and associated technologies have become very popular. We believe that there is now a critical mass to justify a green marketing effort. But to limit risk, we made the decision to slowly add green messaging in order to test the waters.

Green Marketing Principles

Don't let the risks stop you from marketing green. If you have an organization that has started down the green path, in most cases the benefits of telling the world will outweigh the risks. Green marketing is constantly evolving, so you must keep up to date by hiring talent who can tap into the most recent trends. The balance of this chapter will give you some tried-and-true basic green marketing principles to help guide you through marketing green.

Performance and convenience count. Green is not an excuse to get sloppy with products or services. The basics still matter. The green product or service must perform just as well as the nongreen product. So toilet paper made from recycled materials must be as soft and absorbent as the traditional brands that people know and love. The same is true for convenience. A push lawn mower won't take the place of a self-propelled riding mower. Most consumers will not stand for going backwards in convenience. No green marketing program can make up for an ill-conceived green product or service. In fact, after thirty years of poor public perception of green products is finally improving, overcoming images of poorly engineered energy- and water-saving devices from the 1970s energy crisis.

Be authentic. Authenticity is the buzzword in all kinds of marketing, but it is critical in green marketing. Your product or service must have a real environmental benefit. The word "natural" has gotten a bad reputation over the past decade because it has so often been misused to convey bogus green. A toy made from wood may be labeled "natural" (as in "not made from plastic"), but if it is made from wood grown and harvested by forced labor in the rain forest, it's not green at all. Another example is bamboo products, which are often marketed as green. Bamboo is a quickly growing, rapidly renewable fiber (more like a farm crop than a tree), and it seems as if it should be green. But it has also become a lucrative commodity, and in parts of the world workers are cutting down ecologically significant forests to farm bamboo—not so green. A green product or service must be green from every angle to be authentic.

Authenticity also means not overstating the environmental significance of the product or service. Auto companies in Europe have taken heat for claiming that an energy-efficient car is green. Government agencies and watchdog groups counter that any vehicle that runs on nonrenewable fuel and produces pollution is not green.

Tell a story. Green products should tell a story. One of the difficulties with selling green products and services is that people are not knowledgeable enough about environmental issues. In the consumers' defense, environmental benefits can be complicated and confusing. One way to convey the information is through a story for the product or service. You can see this with Fair Trade products. The label or a related website tell where the product was made and may even include a picture of the person who made the product. The label helps get the buyer personally and emotionally involved in the sale. Consumers want their purchases to make them feel good—to turn them into a better person.

My software company's product is not only green but also extremely complicated. So for the past couple of years we have used a story to break down its complexity. We've created a running soap opera with a cast of characters our buyers can relate to—the same personalities, problems, and opportunities. We send out the soap opera installment monthly on a postcard to our prospect list. The installments of the story are on our website so customers, both past and prospective, can catch up. We have won over many a prospect by using this story-based marketing technique. It allows us to convey a complicated list of benefits and product offerings using a story to which people can relate.

Appeal to women. To successfully sell green goods and many earth-friendly services, advertising needs to effectively appeal to women. If you walk the aisles of any natural food store you see the names of women on products: Annie's Naturals, Aimees, Nell's (Nell Newman), and Salsa Lisa, to name a few. The reason is, women buy or influence shopping decisions for over 85 percent of all goods and services. And guess what? They relate to and trust other women. General Mills understood this concept in 1921 when it created Betty Crocker. The company keeps Betty updated by periodically (eight times now) changing her image and keeping her prominent on its goods.

Appealing to women doesn't end with consumer goods: women own 10.4 million businesses in the United States (according to a 2006 estimate by the National Women's Business Council) and make up 47 percent of the work force in the United States. Women are a power to be recognized when selling goods and services to business. It amazes me that women are still so rarely targeted in ads and communications aimed at business. Most business marketers don't realize that green often starts at home and then moves to the office. A 2008 Frank About Women study found that 77 percent of women were either already buying green or will do so if it benefits their family's health. Since we know what is learned at home is also brought to work, business-to-business marketers would be smart to target women at work for purchasing green business goods and services because of their experiences with home products.

Be transparent. There is something in green that begs for honesty. Green marketing must be more than authentic; it must be transparent. When trying to sell green products and services, you must bring forward the good, bad, and ugly to form a bond of trust with your customer. Whether you are marketing a product or service, an effective method is through the organization's website. Writing a blog about various green challenges that relate to your product or service is one way to be transparent. It may seem counterintuitive to discuss negative things about whatever you are trying to sell—a business normally wants to hide those warts. But in the world of green products and services, explaining challenges and how you will fix them can build trust and make your customers more loyal. Although it is rarely done, consumer product companies can gain instant credibility by posting summaries of their third-party audits for their green products on their website.

Appeal to the herd with originality. Use behavior change theory in green marketing efforts. Understand that people do things because their neighbor does it. If people find out that others similar to them are buying a green product or service, they may buy it too. Most people are not leaders or trendsetters. Most want to be in the middle of the herd doing what everyone else is doing. You can see this happen with fashion trends, but the phenomenon goes way beyond fashion to every part of our lives.

Create hip and sexy green messaging. Gone are the days when green was synonymous with ugly and clunky. Green products and services need to rival the appeal of anything else that is being marketed. Beauty and relevance sell green products and services just as well as they sell traditional products and services. Creating an up-to-date image, communications, and sales pitch will also help consumers get past the sins of those awful 1970s green products.

A new marketing trend that is gaining traction is fake authenticity. Organizations that aren't authentically green market their product in a tongue-in-cheek way that will get a green message across but won't bind them so tightly to the concept that they will be accused of greenwashing. A good example of this tactic is the television ad wherein Pat Robertson and Al Sharpton poke fun at each other's politics but unite on needing to do something about global warming—though they admit they don't agree about anything else *(www.wecansolveit.org)*. A product example is a pizza delivery company in Minneapolis that claims to have "planet saving pizza" (can pizza really save the planet?) delivered by caped, masked superheroes in tiny electric cars *(www.galacticpizza.com)*. It is a way to poke fun at the topic but still be able to make strides with green products and services. It plays on the idea that no one, including business, is perfect, but we are still trying to do the right things to improve the world. It is authentic because it reveals our foibles. For more on this topic, read James Gilmore and Joseph Pine II's book, *Authenticity and the Experience Economy.* It is a unique approach to marketing green.

Someone's Watching

When you start to market your company's green initiatives, rest assured someone is paying attention. There are a number of websites and blogs that track corporate behavior. One of these is CorpWatch (www .corpwatch.org), which hands out bimonthly Greenwash Awards (www

.corpwatch.org/article.php?list=type&type=102) to companies who do more to tout their eco-friendliness rather than actually help the environment. Make your green attempts authentic and you won't have to worry about receiving this award.

Sell the green benefit. Green marketers have always struggled with what term to use to convey earth friendliness. I have seen countless permutations of words like green, eco-something, sustainable, efficient, earth-something. Nothing seems to stick as the word or phrase that defines this genre. One strategy that marketing people often focus on is selling the benefit, instead of selling the fact that the product is green. You can sell the benefit by linking the product or service to health and safety (for example, less-toxic cleaning products being safer to use around children). Or you can explain that the benefit is convenience (such as CFL bulbs that need only be changed every million years or so).

Go out and earn some media. There is an opportunity to get earned media for innovative green concepts. Earned media is publicity that can't be purchased. It is news coverage about your business, product, or service from traditional media outlets. The 24/7 media is hungry for good green stories. Many local TV stations are highlighting green as part of their news shows. Local and national papers and magazines often have a day of the week for green. And radio stations are going green all over the country. In late 2007, the NBC peacock was green for a week. Green has become the public service announcement of the late 2000s. If you have an authentic green story to tell, the media will help you tell it. Earned media is almost always more valuable than paid advertising. Let someone else tell your story.

Keeping in mind these principles will help you get the word out in a way that will resonate with the largest number of people. Even though green products and services have been marketed for decades, no one yet has been able to find a single approach that is guaranteed to inspire consumers to action—buy that green product, try that green service, recycle more stuff, change behavior to help stop climate change. Many have tried, but none have figured out the perfect green marketing formula.

What we can figure out is a combination of effective approaches that will create what author Malcolm Gladwell calls "a tipping point." We saw it with smoking cessation campaigns. Through enough effective messaging, the antismoking forces reached a tipping point that resulted in a decline in smoking. We are close to that point of awareness with all things green.

Creating Eco-Legitimacy

A barrier to this tipping point is that there are no universally accepted definitions or standards for what is green. No wonder we are having a tough time inspiring consumers. The problem isn't that standards don't exist. Quite the contrary, there are too many standards and none that are universally accepted. Each program with standards has a graphic or seal with which they mark products or services that have passed their requirements. It's mind-boggling. All of the programs have their strengths and weaknesses, and most are good programs. The problem is confusion among marketing people, who must decide which seal to stick on the package, and among consumers, who must decide which seal they trust. Eventually we will have universally accepted programs, because some of the best minds around the world are working on this labeling issue.

In the meantime, using green experts or spokespeople is another way to lend eco-legitimacy to your product or service and prove that it is verifiably green. Receiving an endorsement from an environmental expert or green-living personality can be an asset in attracting earned media. A spokesperson can also bring green cachet by being able to speak the language of green. Remember that most buyers of consumer products including green consumer products are women. Consider using a female expert or spokesperson who can relate well to your market segment. Product companies and brands that sell sports-related goods often use this technique with sport star endorsements. Likewise, pharmaceutical companies use physicians and researchers in advertisements and earned media to prove that their products are authentic. If you decide to use a spokesperson, hire someone who believes in and uses the product or service. That way you can avoid the charge of greenwashing.

Sustainability reporting or corporate responsibility reporting is another way to prove your eco-legitimacy to the world. A sustainability report is an annual report that gives a holistic view of how the company is doing in the areas of social, economic, and environmental impacts. Public companies are increasingly using this type of messaging as they try to get do-gooder information to stockholders and Wall Street. If you decide to develop a green annual report, be careful to make it more than a marketing piece. In order for it to be effective you must make it transparent and be unafraid to give outsiders a look inside your company. The report should divulge the good, bad, and ugly about the company and products. Several organizations have guidelines for this type of reporting: World Business Council for Sustainable Development (WBCSD), Coalition for Environmentally Responsible Economies (CERES), and the Global Reporting Initiative (GRI).

I have seen this type of annual report used successfully by smaller private organizations. They may not call it a sustainability report, but it has similar elements. The most convincing way to develop a piece like this is to have metrics for environmental improvements and challenges, such as greenhouse gases, energy used, raw materials recycled, and water pollution. The business's stakeholders, environmental groups, and the media can access the information and find out on an annual basis the environmental improvements your company or organization is making.

Another way to transparency through green marketing is to use your organization's website more effectively. Posting your mission, vision, and values is a good start. If someone wants to know what kind of company you aspire to be, they can find out. Consider a blog or video that discusses successes and challenges in going green.

Perhaps the most effective way to truly achieve transparency is to post third-party audits or, at least, summaries of audits—including their criticisms of your company. The American public loves reality TV, particularly reality TV stars who blow it and then show improvement. It's the same with green products and services. It's okay to make mistakes as long as you can show how you are correcting them. We will love you for it. More importantly, we will trust you. True transparency is the pinnacle of any green marketing program.

Easy Steps to Green

Following are four helpful tips to begin marketing a product or service as green. Don't kid yourself, branding green will take all of the creativity and new thinking that you can muster. Authenticity and credibility are difficult to build but essential to success.

1. If You Don't Have It, Hire It

Some people are more creative than others. If you don't have the skill to do your own marketing, don't fake it. Find someone who does. Green marketing is a specialized niche that not every marketing consultant or ad agency can do, so choose carefully. Talk to companies in your area that are advertising green to find out who they have used and if the green marketing advice has resulted in success. Ask a prospective marketing consultant to see the work he or she has previously done with green products or services. Also find out if the consultant has experience in your industry or you may be paying her or him to learn. Don't rule out a national firm that is marketing itself as a green expert. It is possible that a national firm can provide the expertise you need at an affordable price. If you go this route and you are a small business, ask if they deal with other small businesses, and be up-front about your marketing budget.

2. Go to Green Trade Shows

If you are planning to attempt to market your product on your own without a green marketing consultant or agency, hit the green trade show circuit to see how other companies are marketing green. A couple of the larger shows include Natural Products Expo East (*www.expoeast.com*) and USGBC Greenbuild Conference and Expo (*www.greenbuildexpo.org*). Going to a trade show can open your eyes to what works and what doesn't without spending more than the conference fee and some travel expenses. You will find a huge variety of green products and services at the shows, some may be from your same industry. It is a great place to get ideas and ask questions. Trade shows and conferences often include seminars on a wide variety of green business topics including how to market green.

3. Hook Up

If others in your industry are pondering the same question about who to turn to for green marketing help, form a temporary consortium and collaborate to try things or hire an expert. This can take the form of jointly advertising your products or services as green—splitting the costs between several businesses. Or it can simply be an informal brainstorming conversation about how to go about marketing green with colleagues in your industry. Or join a local green business group, if it exists in your area. If there are none, join a national group like Business for Social Responsibility to get green marketing information and contacts.

4. Try Stuff

Another tactic that can work is to experiment on your own. If you are good with words and images, try positioning your own green product or service. Brochure writing, blogs and ad content can be developed with simple off-the-shelf software these days. Use the principles from this chapter to guide your approach and content. You just might hit on something that works for your business. Also don't be afraid to use humor to find the right tone to sell green. Remember the planet saving pizza delivered by the caped crusader? Humor can keep your message positive and memorable.

No matter the marketing approach that you choose, be sure to always practice what you preach. Continue to educate and inspire your market to make your campaign sustainable. Green marketing efforts should be ongoing and not a one time event to be successful. Above all, have fun with anything that you try.

Chapter 13

Pitfalls to Avoid—
Oh, the Mistakes I've Made…

I've made mistakes, but I try to learn something from each blunder. I don't even like to call them mistakes; to me they are do-overs. When you are learning to golf you take a mulligan when you whiff. That's my mindset for green business—most everything is new and experimental. No one has the answers or a perfect formula. Creating a green business is an art and there are no mistakes in art, only creations. One of the most compelling things about green business is that it is new territory, and creative juices get a workout. This is what will keep you engaged over the years as an eco-preneur—you get to create something every day. As long as you stay true to your ethical core and keep your eye on improving the health of the planet, you get to try just about anything.

Let me give you a head start by telling you what I know doesn't work in the world of greening an organization. This will help you quickly move on to trying other things.

Waiting to Get Started

Getting started can be the most difficult part of greening an organization. Many organizations wait for a sign or a trigger signaling that the time is right before they launch a green initiative. They spend a fortune analyzing what their customers want and trying to quantify the benefits. By the time they get the information, it is old and irrelevant because green awareness and progress is moving so swiftly. These wait-and-see-ers don't understand that if the organization initiates an authentic shift in a green direction, there are virtually no negatives. Green is at the core of all things good: efficiency, using resources in a sensible manner, caring, innovation, and love. If done well, greening a business can have incredibly positive results: lower expenses, more profits, happier and healthier people, and more love.

Another excuse is that the business climate isn't right. There may be a recession, tightened credit, or rising expenses. Yet even in times of economic downturn, more businesses than ever are starting to green. There will always be economy-related reasons not to green your business. When times are booming, you are too busy to think about it. When times are difficult, money is too tight and there isn't enough staff. Nothing will ever change if you wait for the perfect moment.

Maybe you're afraid of doing it wrong. You want to make sure you're greening correctly so you can't be criticized. You want assurance that your customers really care if you're offering them a green product. You want a guarantee that you'll save money. You want to know that everyone else is going to do it too.

Well, innovation is messy, and green business is innovation. No one has it down perfectly. In fact, most are just starting down the sustainability path. There is no such thing as perfect when it comes to green—ever. We are all on the spectrum of brown to green and most of us are moving toward green. The worst thing that we can do for our organizations and ourselves is to be paralyzed by this fear of failure.

There is another reason to avoid paralysis. If you don't get your organization thinking and behaving green, the government will do it for you. This has begun on a small scale in some cities that are banning plastic bags. Larger government initiatives include legislating that energy-efficient or green buildings are built in their city. We perhaps do need government to get the laggards to do things that they otherwise would not, but NGOs and business are much better at innovation and creativity than government. I would much rather set a better, higher bar in my own organization, which I can use as a competitive advantage, than have the government legislate what I must do. If you start down this path ahead of government, you can use your ingenuity to find solutions that make good sense and drive innovation and competition in a green direction. Abraham Lincoln said, "The best way to predict your future is to create it." So get creating!

Promoting Responsible Consumption

As you learned in the previous chapter, greenwashing is the purposeful misleading of consumers about the environmental practices of an organization or the environmental benefits of the product or service your organization is selling. Some greenwashing falls in the category of what I call blunderous good intentions: it isn't done to purposely mislead, but unintentionally it deceives the buyer or public. In this case, the product or service for whatever reason can't live up to its green advertising claims or image, because the people creating it didn't know what they were doing.

A second type of greenwashing is *green lite*. The product or service has a green attribute but it isn't green enough to validate the marketing. A bamboo cutting board that was sourced from a once thriving, old-growth tropical forest cut down to make way for a lucrative bamboo plantation is an example of green lite. The product is made with a renewable material, but it's not properly sourced, making it less environmentally friendly than other materials.

Then there is the category of greenwashing that is purposely misleading, attaching itself to the burgeoning green movement for the sole purpose of selling a product or service—*green deception*. An example of this is changing the label on a toxic product to include an image of a forest or other natural scene. This sort of thing is trying to fool the consumer into thinking the product isn't toxic—perhaps even healthy. This type of greenwashing is the most egregious, because it is meant to deceive.

Governments around the world have started to crackdown on greenwashing, ensuring that environmental claims will be scrutinized. Consumers and consumer groups too are aware of greenwashing and often suspicious of companies' green claims. Customers will sometimes treat green marketing with unfair skepticism, in many cases because so many products have been unsubstantiated as green. All companies do not engage in greenwashing, and those that do likely represent a small minority of green products and services.

The best way to avoid greenwashing is to know what you are doing when you are greening a product or service. Engage experts, consumers, NGOs, academics, and trade and professional organizations to help you green. These stakeholders will help you avoid solving one environmental problem at the price of creating another. This type of process will also help you avoid alienating potential allies and benefactors for your product or service.

The other way to bulletproof your organization from greenwashing claims is to make sure that you have a solid foundation of green, that you are not just throwing one green claim or product out there. Be sure to cover your bases by greening parts of your facility, along with your policies, procedures, and people, prior to designing and marketing a green product or service. Use existing standards to substantiate your green claims, or if none exist, develop some measurable standards to demonstrate that what you are doing is rooted firmly in sustainability. The goal of a green business is to promote responsible consumption, not irresponsible or blunderous advertising.

Not Engaging Enviros

An entire network of organizations worldwide have been working on green challenges and solutions for decades—nongovernment organizations (NGOs), environmental nonprofit organizations or enviros. In this country there are tens of thousands of environmental NGOs. There are also an untold number of bloggers, Internet media outlets, and traditional media organizations that focus on communicating all things green, both good and bad. The NGOs have a tremendous amount of experience grappling with all kinds of sustainability issues: water and air pollution, legal issues, product standards, green building, design, carbon credits, climate change, and environmental health, among others. Name any green topic and you can find dozens of NGOs worldwide that are focused on it.

This opens up a tremendous opportunity for businesses looking to green their organizations. The expertise and connections already exist. Reach out and ask for help from an NGO that has similar green goals as yours. A partnership, even if it is informal, can be symbiotic. The business can give the NGO money and exposure to a new audience, while the NGO can help the business thoroughly understand the issues, preventing wasted time and missteps. One caveat: for this to work, the goal of both parties must be to move the green ball forward. It won't work if a business is looking to greenwash its reputation. It also won't work if an NGO is only looking to fill its coffers.

In 2007, a trend began to emerge. Businesses would align with one specific environmental NGO and use that in a public relations campaign. In late 2007, Clorox Company made a deal with the Sierra Club to use their name and logo to market a new line of nonchlorinated cleaning products for an undisclosed fee. This kind of alliance must be considered strategically and carefully by both parties. In some cases, aligning with several NGOs can be better for all organizations in the long run. As with all things green, you should take a systematic approach to making alliances, where inclusivity, as opposed to exclusivity, is critical to your success.

Being Green Obsessed

It doesn't matter whether you are the CEO or janitor of an organization; once you are afflicted with green thinking, you believe that everyone else is too. It is not that green has a religious component, although there are people who believe it does as evidenced by the religious institutions preaching green from the pulpit. Greening can become an obsession because it makes so darn much sense. When I was growing up, my grandmother, who had lived through the Great Depression, couldn't believe we would waste food or throw out clothes that no longer fit. She ran around her house turning out lights after we had left the room. We thought she was, well, cheap. In fact, she was frugal. She couldn't stand to waste anything. In retrospect, she was green.

That is what green does—it makes you realize you should no longer squander anything. As in nature, you should make use of everything, recycling it back into living things, just like decaying leaves on the forest floor fertilize the soil where new trees grow.

Even if you have had a green awakening, realize that others have not had your same "ah-ha" moment of truth. For some, it may take years of exposure to green concepts, because it involves retraining our brains. It is a fundamental change in the way you look at things. Everyone else in the organization probably does not share your green commitment and knowledge. Others need to be brought along.

I have been accused of eco-centriciy greenness many times in my business life. It is not because I'm judgmental about others not being green. It is because I can't fathom that they don't see the world like I do—through green-colored glasses. I guess that I am a bit like my grandmother—she taught me the lesson of avoiding waste. My lifelong challenge has been to bring other people along, while not being impatient with them.

You need to explain things clearly, including the background of why we all need to care. Allow others to catch up on their own terms. Being patient and providing a continuous green stream of information allows others to have their own moment of truth.

Don't Stop Innovating

Are we green enough? Now are we? Now!?! Just when I think that we have hit the pinnacle of sustainability in one of my businesses, I hear of a new technology or new best practices and think, here we go again. There is no such thing as green enough. All organizations and all people fall on a spectrum of green behavior ranging from doing nothing green to doing everything that they can think of that is green. Green perfection is an elusive fantasy. But working toward it is a worthy cause because it provides tangible benefits.

"Continuous improvement" is a phrase probably overused in the business world. It means different things to different industries. In post–WWII Japan, *kaizen* (which translates, roughly, as "continuous improvement") meant improvement by eliminating waste. The Japanese successfully used it to strengthen all functions of business, manufacturing to management. *Kaizen* is often credited for getting Japan back on its feet after the war. If you think about it, our planet's ecosystem is dependent on continuous improvement. In fact, evolution means progression and continuous improvement. In this sense, continuous improvement is critical to our very survival.

It is easy to discuss theories like continuous improvement but more difficult to make them practical. Imagine the greening of your organization as a journey, not a destination. The start of your green business road is a point from which you'll discover ways to continuously improve your performance. The danger of having closed formulas for green—for example, an absolute standard for green products or a rigid certification for green building—is that once it's achieved everybody (raw material providers, manufacturers, retailers and consumers) will sit back and believe this is all the greener they ever have to be. A critical component to green is setting the bar higher and higher, keeping innovation and creativity alive. Just think if Mother Nature stopped innovating at Neanderthal man—we wouldn't be having this discussion.

Zero-Tolerance Policies

A foundation of green and social responsible business is continuous learning. Zero-tolerance policies are a dead end in the world of green and social responsibility. Zero tolerance doesn't allow people to learn from their mistakes. In fact, it can do the opposite and encourage deception. You want to encourage integrity. When there is an enormous penalty for noncompliance with an environmental or social standard, there is a huge incentive to hide mistakes. Many brands and retailers have fallen into this abyss, with zero-tolerance policies for various practices at far-flung factories. Sometimes this results in the closure of a factory, which hundreds of people are depending on for a basic living—all due to a critical code violation.

Zero-tolerance policies should be replaced with a root analysis of the problem. You can then follow this analysis by implementing a solution to correct the reason for the issue. Analysis will explain *why* something is happening, rather than simply identifying the problem. Once you know why a problem such as child labor exists in an organization, you can try to fix it with some coaching and patience. You should couple this approach with very explicit, upfront expectations and a safe environment for workers, so they feel they can report problems without retaliation. Positive progress results when you approach a problem with a solution mentality, not a penalty mentality. If you close a factory, you only encourage more secrecy and hiding of mistakes.

Trying to Do It All at Once

Getting the green bug is a good thing, but true change is incremental and takes time. No one can turn an organization green overnight—no matter how small or how willing the organization. To do it right, green must permeate every part of the organization including the facility, the operation, and the product or service. This can be overwhelming if you don't break it down into bite-sized pieces and spread the work among many hands.

Large organizations such as universities and corporations tend to put one person in charge of sustainability—a green czar. This is a start in the right direction, but it can create problems:

> It can put too much pressure on that person.

> It doesn't properly empower individuals or departments to act in a sustainable way.

> It keeps green power and knowledge in the hands of a few, which is the antithesis of green.

> It encourages others in the organization to let the green czar do all the work.

We made this mistake early on when greening my management firm. Doug was our green czar and responsible for getting agreement from the rest of the people in the company. He had the responsibility to keep us green, but we gave him no true power to do so. After a while Doug was seen as the pesky green guy who was making everyone's job harder because of his crazy suggestions—at least, lots of employees thought they were crazy. It is critical to find a way to make everyone in the company a green czar, not just one person.

Not Enough Agreement

No matter how green an organization becomes, getting agreement and commitment from the new and uninformed within your ranks is a perennial challenge. You need a critical mass of people doing green things to sustain the effort. An ongoing indoctrination of the new and unconverted is essential.

This is not a prescription for a cult; it is simple organizational theory. To effect lasting change, there are some principles to remember:

Allow people to learn about green. Green information isn't poured into people; they learn it by experimenting with it. Getting agreement requires that both heart and mind are involved. Set up teams to brainstorm and try out green ideas. Allow people to have ownership and pride in their own progress and programs.

Give concrete, measurable goals. Give targets for people and departments to shoot for so that they have measurable goals. Start with simple things, like reducing the number of reams of paper from month to month or reducing the electric bill. The important thing is to give targets and then keep measuring. What gets measured gets accomplished.

Assign responsibility. Use people who have a track record of leadership to help you green. Let them know that you are counting on them to inspire new green behavior and that they have your confidence. Give them the responsibility and the power to make the changes that need to be made—resist micromanaging change.

Give out green rewards. Develop a reward system for good green behavior. Make it a part of the review process and give raises based on implementing green ideas. Run green contests to keep it at the top of everyone's minds.

Keep the vision up front and center. Keep repeating the green messages until everyone in the organization can explain it in their sleep. Have green messaging posted in visible locations. Constantly work it. It should become a mantra for everyone in the organization.

Hogging Green Knowledge

Green progress belongs to the planet and it is begging to be shared. Yes, you may have developed a proprietary formula for converting algae into free energy and you want to keep that formula a secret. But most green solutions are not proprietary and would do the world and your organization good if you shared the information. That is not to say that you can't make money with green ideas. You can. Green businesses have made plenty of money on green ideas and will continue to do so as green products and services become more mainstream.

There are some real benefits to sharing how you were able to green your product, service, facility, or operations. You will be considered a leader and expert, because every organization is struggling with how to do this. You will also no longer be alone, and you will learn from others in your industry how to move green further along, saving money and resources and reducing your environmental impact. If you share your successes and failures, you also may be able to influence public policy.

There are many organizations you can join to share your green knowledge. Most trade and professional organizations have a green group working through sustainability issues. Join one that interests you. If there is not a group, form one.

Underestimating the Power of Green

Many businesspeople don't totally get the potency of being earth friendly. They may understand that there is some money to be saved in efficiency initiatives or that greening a product or service could be a moneymaking proposition somewhere down the road. They may even recognize that it is the right thing to do, but few know the massive power that can be harnessed when the organization makes a conscious effort to embrace sustainability. A good cause can harness both the hearts and minds of people, and that, my friends, can move mountains!

The reason that green is so potent is that many people today crave meaning in their work lives. More and more, young workers won't settle for just a paycheck. They feel they have the right to meaningful work as well. Working toward being a more resource efficient, health-conscious, and caring organization can ignite a fiery passion in people. You can see the difference between an organization where people are fulfilled with their work and contagiously happy and one where they just go through the motions. Greening the organization gives people a passion and a purpose. It grants them powers to change the world.

Green can make any organization better. It has the power to enhance the work experience by changing the focus to something that nearly everyone values and can get behind—the planet that sustains us. Unlike other causes, which may be targeted toward a limited segment of the population, taking care of the environment is universal. On some level, we all understand that our survival hinges on what we do in our working lives and how we do it. Greening has the power to provide purpose and in so doing make us feel happier and more fulfilled. It boils down to allowing people to bring their feelings and whole selves to work. Giving employees the opportunity to contribute to a universal cause is a gift all organizations can offer simply by starting to green their business.

Chapter 14

Getting Started—
a Kick in the Green Jeans

If you are like me, you sometimes read the last chapter of a book first to find out how the story ends. So I have written the last chapter to be an executive summary rather than a typical last chapter. It will hopefully give you a bird's-eye view of green business, so you don't get lost in the trees. Even though I have talked about the information in this book hundreds of times to my own companies, consulting with other companies, and in speeches around the country, I am surprised at the volume of material that I have created. And I am afraid that it gives the wrong impression—that greening an organization is backbreaking work.

I don't want to leave you with this impression, because the work level is one reason organizations sometimes don't begin green initiatives. Companies can have the information, the talent, and even the money to begin greening, but they don't do it because they don't have the time. We are all hyper-busy, and adding one more responsibility to an overflowing to-do list is not appealing. In fact, I have found that my message can occasionally make people want to run from the room screaming, "You are now making saving the planet part of my job description? On top of everything else?!?"

Let's put an end to this misconception right now. Greening is not backbreaking work. It involves work, but so does any other change or improvement. Green is no different. In its simplest form, greening is about organizational and behavioral change. The only thing different is that green is holistic and inclusive by definition, so the work tends to be collaborative, with many hands and minds lightening the load.

Having founded five companies, I know that building a company is backbreaking work. It involves planning, finding money, finding clients, hiring, firing, competing, and marketing. Every waking (and sometimes sleeping) hour is consumed with building the organization. And that goes on for years. After a particularly difficult situation, my CEO and I look at each other and agree, "If running a business were easy, everyone would do it." As rewarding as it can be, business is often hard work, emotionally and physically.

On the other hand, greening a company is a blast. You get to tweak and improve what you have already built or are in the process of building. You look at the same old products, your workspace, and your staff from a fresh perspective, asking how you and your company can do it better. Greening is not competitive or painful; instead it is a rare pleasure in the working world. It is downright fulfilling:

> One reason for that is the world wants more green and everything is conspiring toward that end.

> People have a thirst for meaning in their work lives, and green provides it.

> We have begun to care about the planet that sustains us.

Hands down, working toward sustainability is the best decision that I've made in my twenty-five-plus-year career.

If I haven't yet convinced you in this summary to start greening your organization, read or reread Chapter 1. You'll find the urge to green your business irresistible. If you have read the entire book, I assume that you want to go for the green. Well, here is your summary of how to do it—the magic formula for how to green your business and make it stick. Well, okay, so maybe it's not exactly magic (my lawyer hates it when I make promises in writing he hasn't reviewed). But the formula has worked for me. I didn't use this with my very first business that I greened, because I hadn't yet had all of the experiences that brought me to this point. I am constantly tweaking this process as I find new things that work. So my prescription constantly gets better.

Here are my steps for greening:

Step #1: Be It to See It

The best way to experiment with green is to start at home. It's like putting on a new pair of glasses with green lenses. Before you do anything, first see and think green. As you go through your weekend or weekday routine, ask green questions. Each time you go to the garbage can ask, "Shall I throw it or can I recycle it?" Each time you get in the car ask, "Can I combine this trip with another nearby errand?" At the grocery store ask, "Can I find the same or similar product in bulk?" In the yard ask, "Can I find a way to use less water or mow less or quit using toxic chemicals?" At the ATM machine ask, "Do I really need the receipt?"

Those of us who have been around since the 1970s environmental movement have some green emotional baggage. We tend to think that being green means sacrifice and going without modern convenience, but that kind of thinking went out with President Jimmy Carter's cardigan (no offense; at the time, he looked good in the cardigan). Today, being green at home means doing things more efficiently and comfortably while saving money and resources. It also involves being healthier and happier.

Psychologists are now calling worry about the environment "eco-anxiety." The only way to cure this anxiety, other than popping pills or drinking heavily, is to do something positive for the environment. Take one step by recycling, which will help the planet one product at a time. Then, you can apply that at work. Organic gardening is a good release for this eco-anxiety, and it, too, is good way to learn about what can be done at work.

Once you have done some experimenting with greening your home, start thinking about how you might engage in this same behavior at work. Odds are that you are already doing plenty at home and are ready to dive into some kind of green program in your organization. If you start talking about your green efforts at work, this may encourage others to start experimenting with their own green initiatives at home and at work.

Step #2: Engage in Sustainability Thinking

I use the terms green and sustainability interchangeably through this book, but don't ignore the bigger picture of sustainability even when I use the term green. Sustainability is care for the environment in addition to consideration for social and economic impacts. All three elements: people, planet, and profit must be present and in balance for an organization to be sustainable.

It's often said that sustainability is meeting the needs of the current generation without compromising the needs of future generations. It is the golden rule: Do unto others as you would have them do unto you. Sustainability implies that all people and the entire ecosystem must be treated with love and respect. In order for your organization to be successful with greening, you must make sustainability the basis for all your actions. A green organization that pays no attention to the costs and savings won't be around very long. Neither will a profitable green products organization that treats its staff horribly or alienates the community in which it operates. People, profitability, and the planet are all inextricably linked in a green business.

The best way to incorporate sustainability thinking into your business is to first green your corporate governance. To do this effectively, you should go through a strategic planning process so that the mission, vision, and values statements of your company are created or changed to reflect a sustainability commitment. When green initiatives are in the works, it pays to do planning and go back to basics. Everyone in an organization needs to be on the same page for a green plan to be successful. Green must permeate the heart and soul of an organization to be lasting. The best way to do this is to make it the core of the organization's public and private "who we are" statements. If sustainability is not part of your company's current vision, mission, or values, change them.

Step #3: Collaborate

Gather assistance from many fronts to carry out your green initiatives. There are plenty of people and organizations just waiting for your call. Realize that most local governments have a staff of people working on green improvements in the community, and they would jump at the opportunity to partner with a company to move their agenda along. The same is true with nonprofit environmental organizations or NGOs that have been working on the same environmental challenges for years. They, too, might welcome a well-intentioned company that has begun to focus on the same issue, only this time from a business perspective.

Start networking with local city and county officials. They can help you find NGOs that are working on various environmental concerns. Find overlapping areas of interest, and ask if they have materials that you can use or if you can be a demonstration project for them. Any collaborative project must first and foremost provide a direct benefit to the environment. Partnering allows you to share resources and limit duplication of effort, as long as you share the same end goal of environmental improvement.

My companies have partnered successfully in this manner countless times. It works best if the issue has a limited scope. Once we partnered with a nonprofit organization that was doing demonstration projects, promoting responsible water management through native landscaping techniques. They used several of our townhome communities under management and found public grants to do 50 percent of the work. The properties happily matched funds and in return had a new, beautiful wildlife habitat area that is maintained with very little water or chemicals. The nonprofit took pictures and sent others interested in planting their own native area to the property. My management firm looked good because it was promoting an environmentally sound way to landscape. It was a golden opportunity to teach by example, and the relationship was win-win for everyone involved.

We formed a completely different kind of informal partnership with the county's solid waste management board in the late 1990s. They wanted to do a demonstration of an office that was trying to use less paper. We agreed to take this on and were given a consultant hired by the waste management board that taught us to measure and track our paper use. Part of the deal was that we had to match the funds with our own staff time to track ongoing paper use and the associated staff costs. It was well worth the investment because the study enabled us to realize how expensive it was to move paper. The process helped us take the first steps to automate and begin using less paper. The county obtained statistics about paper use and developed a demonstration case. Again, it was a win-win situation. My firm became more paperless through a consultant we wouldn't have otherwise hired, and it gave the board a way to push their agenda of reducing business waste.

Don't limit your thinking to government and nonprofit groups. Sometimes the best collaborative partners are found right in your own industry—your competition. Forming an industry group to share information and work out the kinks in environmental challenges can be another good and inexpensive solution. You can do this through a trade or professional association or just by picking up the phone and calling someone in a company who has a role similar to yours. The key to this kind of collaboration is to make sure that people are comfortable enough to share. Contact a nearby college or university as another way to find willing and able collaborators. In some cases, you can match your needs to a professor or student's interests and achieve an otherwise impossible feat with someone who has a vast knowledge in a green area of expertise, like design, architecture, or engineering.

Make time to brainstorm about how you can collaborate and who would make a good partner to help you achieve your green goals. The collaborations can be for a fixed period of time while you complete a project, or they can be ongoing through the life of an initiative. Collaborators can also form an ongoing advisory board for the green initiative in your organization. Once you have done several collaborations, you begin to build up a credible list of allies to whom you can go for advice and counsel on other green matters. Collaborating regularly will also help you broaden your base of support, which will ultimately help you lighten the load. The point is, you don't need to go it alone. If you look for overlapping goals with other organizations and causes, it can produce odd green bedfellows that get things done.

Step #4: Map It Out

When I was a teenager I worked in a wilderness area in the summer as an assistant guide. If we were temporarily disoriented or lost, the rule was if you can figure out where you are, you can always find where you are going. It worked because if you could locate yourself on the map, you could always find your way back to the base camp. This applies as well to greening an organization: If you know what you've already done, you will know what you have left to do. That is why I recommend using a green gap analysis (G-Gap) early on in your quest to green. A green gap analysis is an assessment tool that helps you identify the gap between what green things you are currently doing and what green things you could consider doing. It can help you create a prioritized list of green business possibilities.

A G-Gap can be a very sophisticated exercise. You can compile and compare various metrics broken down by business function such as human resources, finance, product, marketing, and so on. But, don't let this step bog you down. It should be a quick and dirty checklist, showing what you have done and which areas you should tackle next. It is a basic roadmap to green your organization.

Divide a spreadsheet into the three areas that can be greened in any organization: the facility, the operation, and the product or service. Make a list of the things that have already been greened by accident or on purpose in your organization. Yes, even accidental greening counts. What matters is that it is already done. Once that is identified, you can figure out what you have left to do in each category.

The list for every organization is different, and you should customize it to fit your needs. Appendix B has a prototype for a G-Gap, but use it only as a starting point or guide. As you look at the list of green possibilities, you will see that the prototype is very general but can easily be made specific to your industry by adding the specifics of product or service design, sourcing, and distribution line items.

After you have identified what you have already done to go green, decide what is left to do. To develop your green wish list, assemble a team to put together a green plan of attack. Ideally, this group will consist of various stakeholders including owners, shareholders, management team, employees, vendors, customers, and subcontractors. This can work whether you are a sole proprietor or have hundreds of employees, as long as you limit the group to a size that is workable.

Step #5: Find the Low-Hanging Fruit

When you begin to green an organization, keeping it simple is key to building enthusiasm and traction. Target a few areas that are easily achievable and visible to your inside constituents. While these areas will vary by industry, usually the facility is a good place to ensure some early success. There are plenty of green building case studies and many well-developed products and techniques that can be applied to any office suite, manufacturing plant, or retail operation, no matter what their size. Focusing first on improving energy efficiency will also get you moving in the right direction of reducing your own carbon footprint and greenhouse gas output, all the while saving the organization money. An added benefit of starting here is that energy savings are easily quantifiable through utility bills.

Another easy area to tackle is toxic product usage. This should be on the list for early implementation. The results and the pay-back period are not so accurately measurable, but dealing with the problem will send a message to your staff that you care and that you are concerned about their health and safety.

The next areas that lend themselves well to beginning to green are people, policies, and practices: the operation. It can take some time to get your staff educated and enthusiastic about greening, so starting early is a good idea. Develop a green team, or green teams, so that employees can discuss and compete based on their green contributions at work and at home. Make it fun. Hold contests to get the green mentality going. People will make green changes if their coworkers are doing it. Involve the early adaptors and leaders in your organization, and the rest will follow their green example.

Greening the product or service should also be on the top half of your G-Gap sheet. Greening a product or service usually takes the most time and effort; however, this is also where the biggest financial reward potential is found. It takes patience and time to change a traditional product or service into an authentically green one. There will almost certainly be a learning curve, not only for your organization but also for your customer. Customers, like the rest of us, can be adverse to change and slow to adopt anything new and different. If your product or service is one of the first in the industry to be greened, it may take lots of education before you can make the big sales. Getting a group of clients together in a user group to discuss possible changes in the product or service is a good way to help you formulate later marketing and sales tactics.

A mistake that some make when launching a green product or service is to concentrate on the end product, ignoring everything that happens in between. The design and manufacturing may be where most of your resources can be saved or squandered. It won't matter how much environmental design went into the product if the factory that makes the product wastes precious resources or acquires materials and labor from illegal or unsustainable sources. You must enforce ethical supply-chain management and environmental management systems, regardless of where the product is produced.

It is usually best to make sure that initiatives involve both the facility and operation in addition to greening your product before you release a lot of information to the public. Make sure you are green enough before you officially launch. Green enough is a very subjective concept. Test your concept of green with insiders, customers, and some NGO friends before you do a full-scale green product or service launch.

Step #6: Bulletproof It

Some day, green businesses will be the rule rather than the exception. Until then, skeptics may question whether your business or your product is green enough. If you're an early adopter in your industry, some may accuse you of greenwashing or, worse yet, of being wrong in your implementation of green strategies.

Eventually there will be universally recognized green standards for each industry and for all product categories and services. Currently, there are widely accepted standards for some industries (for example, what makes a building green from the U.S. Green Building Council). Various product standards crop up around the globe such as the USDA Organic standard. Perhaps in time the chamber of commerce or Business for Social Responsibility will venture into the green business certification arena as green businesses become more pervasive.

Although such universally accepted standards and certifications will increase green business credibility, they also may curtail sustainability progress. In the years before sustainability became a widespread philosophy, the government set a low bar for environmental laws. Many businesses settled for minimal compliance rather than striving to become more green. Universally accepted standards for a green business could create a new least common denominator, and some organizations will settle for meeting, rather than exceeding, those standards.

To avoid this, organizations must strive for a higher and higher level of green even as standards become prevalent. The secret to true organizational green credibility involves three essential elements: standards, audits, and transparency. If your organization can provide all three of these critical components, it will earn a green reputation.

This sounds magical, but how does this work in the real world? The first thing you can do is check around to find out if there are any environmental or social standards that already exist for your product, service, or industry. If there are standards, find out what it takes to meet them. If there is a certification process in place, develop a plan to become certified. If formal certification is economically beyond your reach, due to fees, draw up a plan to meet the standards anyway. There can still be value in meeting or exceeding published standards, even though you cannot display the certification logo.

In the absence of recognized green standards, develop your own. Your standards may be more stringent and creative than those others would create. If you take the time and energy to develop good standards, they may eventually become the basis for the industry or product standard. You need to think of it as an opportunity to expand the world of green. In my property management firm, we are in the process of developing our own sustainability standards because none exist for the management of homeowner communities or common interest communities. We are assembling a team of NGOs, fellow management firms, and government agency representatives to accomplish this. We will use the standards and hope that other property management companies will use them as well. Perhaps someday our work will be used to develop a green national standard and accreditation for this type of property.

Once there is a standard in place, have a third party audit your progress against the standard. This is the second key to green authenticity. At the risk of stating the obvious, standards need to be measurable. A standard that cannot be measured cannot be audited in an objective way. The third-party auditor should be someone who is independent from and not associated with your business in any manner. Typically, accounting or engineering companies are capable of doing audits. The independent auditor will make sure that you are meeting or exceeding the standard by visiting the site where your product or service is being manufactured or performed. Depending on the standard, this may be an audit of the entire supply chain or just one supplier in the chain. Once the audit is complete, you will receive a written report to notify you if you are in compliance with the standard. If there are some areas not in compliance, you will be given a window of opportunity to improve before the auditor returns. Using third-party auditors makes a statement that you are serious about meeting the green standard, whether it is your own or was developed by a certifying entity.

The third key ingredient to green authenticity is transparency. Transparency means letting it all hang out—not just the good stuff, but your organizational warts too. We all want to put our best foot forward, particularly if we are trying to sell something. Businesses often don't talk about the negatives for fear no one will want what they are selling. But to gain green credibility, it is important to tell the good, the bad, and the ugly. It may seem counterintuitive, but disclosing your challenges can work to your benefit and can actually help you sell by making you more trustworthy. Devoting a portion of your company website to your standards, audit summaries, and solutions to your green challenges can make you believable and authentically green. It can also help others in your industry understand and improve upon solutions to green obstacles. And it will differentiate you from your competitors, who may be telling a less believable green story.

Step #7: Communicate, Communicate

Within your organization, tell everyone what you are going to do to be green, and then tell everyone what you did. Tell them again and again and again. This is a must when you are greening an organization. It is the only way to keep everybody within the organization mindful of the goal to be sustainable.

Sustainability is not instinctive at this point in human history. Long ago, when we were living off the land farming, hunting, and gathering, everyone was in tune with the cycles of nature, the rhythms of the weather, and the flora and fauna because their lives depended upon it. Not so today. Most of us live in cities and in buildings completely insulated from any care about the weather or anything else. We need to be reminded that we are part of the ecosystem, not separate from it. We need to be reminded so that we relearn what was programmed out of us as a species over the past couple of centuries. We need to learn to think with the ecosystem in mind. Relearning on that scale takes some effort and lots of communication.

There are many ways to communicate, and you may need to try lots of things to find out what works for the people in your organization. I am often asked to speak at companies and trade and professional conferences to try to get people energized about the possibilities of greening. It is getting easier to connect with people on this issue because the media has become so engaged with the topic. We constantly hear about green in every kind of media, but we are still far from the eco-centric thinking of our ancestors.

Communicate often and with vigor. Events held only once a year won't bring about the shift that an organization needs to be authentically green. You must make continuous efforts throughout the year. You must embed sustainability into every speech, every event, every communication, every celebration, and every meeting. The organization should be overflowing with green in every person, department, and direction.

Step #8: Expect Good Things

Once you have begun to green your business by following steps one through seven, you will be well on your way to creating a new kind of organization. You won't see all of the benefits raining down on you at once, but slowly, if you are keeping track, you should begin to notice your expenses decreasing—or at least not increasing as exponentially as they otherwise would given the prices of resources and energy. You may also find your revenue increasing if you green part of your product line or services. You will find that deep green consumers are exceptionally loyal and will, at times, pay a premium to be reassured that what you are selling is human healthy and planet friendly.

If you have been continuously and effectively engaging your staff in green and monitoring their behavior, you will find that they are taking fewer sick days and enjoying their work more. Employees are happier, because they can sometimes telecommute or work flexible days. There is talk at lunchtime or during meetings about how the organization can be even greener, saving more resources and automating more. There is a new, positive feeling in the business that you can't quite put your finger on exactly. People just seem more enthusiastic about their work.

Your competition has started to notice that you are doing something new. They are skeptical about your greening, but they are watching you with interest. Perhaps they are even jealous that you are greening your facility or product. In fact, one of their key people called you the other day to see if you were hiring. She wants to work for a company that is doing positive things for the environment. And the media has noticed too. You received a call from the local newspaper asking about your four-day workweek that helps employees save gas and cut down on greenhouse emissions.

For the first time in a long time, you feel energized and good about going to work in the morning. You look at your kids and think that the work you are doing will make the world a better place for them. There is no longer a knot in your stomach when you think about the volume of waste your company creates or the greenhouse gases emitted when manufacturing your products. You are even sleeping better at night knowing that you and your company have decided to stop being part of the problem and started becoming part of the solution. And when you realize that greening can equal success and profit, you will smile.

All of these things and many more are possible when you embark on the journey to green a business. When young people ask me what work they can do to save the environment, I ask them in what ways they live green in their own home and at work. They realize they can make a huge difference by helping to create green solutions for their current workplace. They don't all have to work as environmental engineers or for a company that is making a green product to contribute. We need everyone involved in every type of business and organization. Greening gives anyone who owns, operates, or works in a business a meaningful mission for an entire career. There is much to do in this new green business revolution, and the time is now. Take that first green business step and keep on going. I'll see you on the path.

Appendix A

Resources

Internet
Green Building Maintenance

Green Cleaning Network: *www.GreenCleaningNetwork.org*

Environmental Choice: *www.EnvironmentalChoice.com*

EPA's Comprehensive Procurement Guidelines: *www.epa.gov/cpg*

Integrated pest control: *www.green.ca.gov/EPP/building/structipm.htm*

Environmental Protection Agency: *www.epa.gov/pesticides/factsheets/ipm.htm*

American Lung Association (resources for air freshners): *www.lungusa.org/site/apps/lk/links.aspx?c=dvLUK9O0E&b=35994*

University of Minnesota Extension office (clean indoor air): *www.extension.umn.edu/yardandgarden/ygbriefs/h110indoorair.html*

National Institute of Environmental Health (health information on air fresheners): *www.niehs.nih.gov/news/releases/2006/airfreshener.cfm*

EPA Energy Star program (lighting and office equipment): *www.energystar.gov*

Illuminating Engineering Society of North America: *www.iesna.org*

Green Building

American Council for an Energy Efficient Economy—HVAC information: *www.aceee.org/ogeece/ch3_index.htm*

Resource Center for green building: *www.greenerbuildings.com*

U.S. Green Building Council (LEED): *www.usgbc.org*

Forest Stewardship Council: *www.fsc.org*

The Green Building Initiative: *www.thegbi.org/greenglobes/*

Natural Resources Defense Council (sustainable construction benefits): *www.nrdc.org/buildinggreen/bizcase/default.asp*

Green Spaces

Sustainable Sites Initiative (sustainable landscaping): *www.sustainablesites.org*

EarthEasy (xeriscaping information): *www.eartheasy.com/grow_xeriscape.htm*

Green Builder (greywater irrigation information): *www.green builder.com/sourcebook/greywater.html*

Greenroofs (green roofing solutions): *www.greenroofs.com*

Green Operation

Green Money Journal: *www.greenmoney.com*

Earth 911 (recycle anything, organized by zip code): *www.Earth911.org*

Climate Biz (business resource for climate management): *www.climatebiz.com*

Ecopreneurship.com (advice on social entrepreneurship): *www.ecopreneurship.com*

Green Biz.com (green business clearinghouse of information): *www.greenbiz.com*

Green Transportation

Environmental Protection Agency SmartWay: *www.epa.gov/smartway*

Business for Social Responsibility (includes the Clean Cargo Working Group): *www.bsr.org/membership/working-groups.cfm*

Green Products and Services

Carbon Disclosure Project: *www.cdproject.net*

Biomimicry (information for product design): *www.biomimicry.org*

Centre for Sustainable Design: *www.cfsd.org.uk*

Entirely Sustainable Product Design (includes green design checklist): *www.espdesign.org*

GreenBlue Institute (sustainable design information): *www.greenblue.org*

Scientific Certifications Systems: *www.scscertified.com*

Green Seal (certification programs): *www.greenseal.org*

Consumer Reports Greener Choices (information on green products): *www.greenerchoices.org*

Green Packaging

Ecopackaging.net (resource for sustainable packaging): *www .ecopackaging.net*

Sustainable Packaging Coalition: *www.sustainablepackaging.org*

Sustainable Packaging Task Group (subgroup of the Institute of Packaging Professionals): *www.iopp.org*

Biopolymer.net (bioplastics information): *www.biopolymer.net*

Green Marketing

U.S. Federal Marketing Guidelines: *www.ftc.gov/bcp/grnrule/ guides980427.htm*

Global Reporting Initiative: *www.globalreporting.org*

Sustainable Packaging Is Good (sustainable innovation in marketing and branding): *www.sustainableisgood.com*

Lifestyles of Health and Sustainability (LOHAS market information): *www.lohas.com*

Treehugger (consumer site): *www.treehugger.com*

General Green Business

Business for Social Responsibility: *www.bsr.org*

World Business Council for Sustainable Development: *www.wbcsd.org*

Corporate Socially Responsible (news service): *www.CSRwire.com*

Green Business (clearinghouse of information): *www.greenbiz.com*

Magazines Related to Green Business

E/The Environmental Magazine (*www.emagazine.com*)
green@work (*www.greenatworkmag.com*)
Package Design Magazine (*www.packagedesignmag.co*m)
Sustainable Industries (*www.sustainableindustries.com*)

Selected Green Books

Anderson, Ray. *Mid-Course Correction: Toward a Sustainable Enterprise: The Interface Model.* (White River Junction, VT: Chelsea Green Publishing, 1998).

Benyus, Janine. *Biomimicry: Innovation Inspired by Nature.* (New York, NY: HarperCollins, 1997).

Brown, Lester. *Eco-Economy.* (New York, NY: W.W. Norton & Company, Inc, 2001).

Brown, Lester. *Plan B Rescuing: A Planet under Stress and a Civilization in Trouble.* (New York, NY: W.W.Norton & Company, Inc, 2003).

Brower PhD, Michael and Warren Leon PhD. *The Consumer's Guide to Effective Environmental Choices.* (New York, NY: Three Rivers Press, 1999).

Carson, Rachel. *Silent Spring.* (New York, NY: Houghton Mifflin Company, 1962).

Colborn, Theo, Dianne Dumanoski, and John Peterson Myers. *Our Stolen Future.* (New York, NY: Penguin Group, 1996).

Elkinton, John. *Cannibals with Forks: The Triple Bottom Line of 21st Century Business.* (Oxford: Capstone Publishing, 1997).

Gould, Kira and Lance Hosey. *Women in Green: Voices of Sustainable Design.* (Bainbridge Island, WA: Ecotone Publishing Company, 2007).

Hawken, Paul. *The Ecology of Commerce.* (New York, NY: HarperCollins, 1993).

Makower, Joel and Business for Social Responsibility. *Beyond the Bottom Line: Putting Social Responsibility to Work for Your Business and the World.* (New York, NY: Simon and Schuster, 1994).

McDonough, William and Michael Braungart. *Cradle to Cradle.* (New York, NY: North Point Press, 2002).

Ray PhD, Paul and Sherry Ruth Anderson PhD. *The Cultural Creatives* (New York, NY: Harmony Books, 2000).

Weisman, Alan. *The World Without Us.* (New York, NY: Thomas Dunne Books, 2007).

Appendix B

Checklists and Surveys

Building Occupant Comfort Survey

1. Is your workspace drafty, too hot, or too cold?
2. Does the air seem stale or have a moldy smell?
3. Do you have headaches, burning eyes, or a feeling of general low energy that clears up while you are away from the building?
4. Is the lighting sufficient for doing your job?
5. Would you like more or less lighting?
6. Are there empty rooms with lights on?
7. Are the bathrooms clean?
8. Can you smell strong cleaning product odors in the bathrooms in the morning?
9. Does your building have new carpet or paint odor?
10. Is your area at high risk for radon?

Summary of Green Building Considerations

General Green Building

> Durable materials are better: spreading the capital cost over more years means cheaper life cycle cost.

> Design to eliminate common health hazards: radon, mold, and poisons.

> Design for recycling: make it easy for occupants to recycle by providing space for them to do so and convenient pickup areas for recyclers.

> Less is more: streamline square-footage needs based on function and utility rather than ego and rank.

> Minimize construction waste: design around standard sized building materials.

> Construct with recycled and recyclable materials.

> Don't dump: practice deconstruction when remodeling or building out new space.

Site Considerations

> Recycle an existing building

> Locate near mass transit

> Angle building for passive solar advantages

> Locate in high employee density areas

> Always preserve wildlife habitat and wetlands

> Locate on a brownfield site

> Limit nonpermeable surfaces like asphalt parking lots

> Provide on-site storm water management

> Install water efficient irrigation

> Landscape for minimal maintenance and inputs

Materials Considerations

> Low maintenance

> Rapidly renewable

> Durable

> Reclaimed and salvaged

> Certified sustainable wood and other green certified materials as they become available

> Recycled and recyclable

> Locally produced, harvested, or mined

> Not chemically treated

> Packaged minimally

Aim for Energy and Resource Efficiency

> Use high-efficiency HVAC equipment

> Have on-site renewable energy capabilities

> Install water and electric saving sensors and controls

> Recycle on-site

> Take advantage of natural light wherever possible

> Purchase green power

Improve Indoor Space Quality

> Nonpetroleum-based decorating

> Low-emitting building materials

> Fresh air intake

> Plants

> Air purifiers

> Thermal comfort

Green Gap Analysis

This is only an example. This type of questionnaire must be customized.

Inside Space

Are less-toxic cleaning practices used?

Is integrated pest management practiced?

Are there policies for thermostat control?

Is cleaning done during business hours?

Is there a power strip policy that is enforced?

Are there lighting occupancy sensors?

Has the HVAC been recommissioned?

Is there a monthly checklist for HVAC that is used?

Has an occupancy comfort survey been done?

Is there a plan for deconstruction when space is remodeled?

Is a green roof a possibility?

Outside Space

Does rain water run off the property?

Is best use made of hard surface parking?

Are permeable or semipermeable materials used for hard surfaces?

Are there rain gardens?

Is there adequate green space with minimal turf?

Is there a policy in place to use more efficient lawn equipment?

Is xeriscaping used?

Are organics used for turf and gardens?

Is drip irrigation used?

Is there a graywater system for irrigation?

Transportation

Is there a green parking plan?

Is there a car-sharing hub on site or nearby?

Is there a bicycle corral?

Does the organization subsidize or encourage the use of mass transit?

Are company-owned vehicles energy efficient?

Is telecommuting allowed and encouraged for some staff?

Is a four-day workweek allowed?

Are online meetings used instead of travel whenever possible?

Operation

Is the amount of office paper purchased decreasing?

Is there an online document management system?

Are the accounts receivable and payable paperless?

Can company inquiries be made online?

Are promotional materials minimized?

Is there postconsumer content in all office paper?

Has vendor packaging been reduced?

Are you a member of a recycled material exchange program?

Are the bottles, cans, paper, and electronics recycled?

Employees

Is there a green component to the vision/mission/values of the organization?

Are there SRI options for 401(k) or retirement accounts?

Does the company subsidize any green behavior at home?

Is there paid time off for green volunteerism?

Is there green criteria for hiring?

Are employees encouraged to report problems?

Are green goal achievements part of the employee review process?

Is there ongoing green education for employees?

Does the company practice green meetings?

Is there a no-fragrance policy?

Is there a green IT plan for computer equipment?

Are green rewards institutionalized?

Product or Service

Are products sourced via ethical sourcing methodology?

Are any segments of the supply chain green?

Is there an environmental management plan in place?

Are there environmental certification programs that are being used?

Are there sustainability product or service standards that are being enforced?

Is there a code of conduct for both social and environmental standards?

Are green design principles being used?

Are sustainable packaging principles being applied?

Are third-party audits taking place?

Are audit summaries posted for the public?

Is green messaging accurate and authentic?

Is responsible consumption encouraged?

Is there sustainability reporting?

Index

About the Author

Often credited for tirelessly working to preserve our planet long before global warming hit the mainstream radar, Kim Carlson is an eco-savvy entrepreneur, green business author, and eco-chic lifestyle expert. She is the founder of five successful companies that use earth-friendliness as their driving force. Her latest venture is the development of the EarthSmart Product Standard, a retail product certification program devised in collaboration with the country's leading scientists, academics, and environmentalists that will prove to be the most innovative environmental screening process to date.

Carlson practices what she preaches. (Except she doesn't really preach, she enthuses.) For more than twenty years, she has been a high-profile, socially responsible business leader, eco-preneur, and activist called upon to consult for corporations, universities, governments, and consumer groups. She has worked with politicians and policy makers as chair of the Minnesota Environmental Initiative, a member of the Governors Roundtable for Sustainability, and as a Public Policy Forum Fellow at the Humphrey Institute of the University of Minnesota. Carlson was a pioneer in the green housing movement in the early 90s, which subsequently has become a major national phenomenon. She is also the founder of five companies that use earth-friendliness as their driving force and serves as a board member for six nonprofit environmental organizations. Carlson's EarthSmart Consumer Test—designed for consumers to discover how green their lifestyle is—has become a buzzed-about benchmark of green living.

As the "EarthSmart Expert" on NBC, the host of the national radio program *Livin' The Green Life*, and the regular guest writer for the Minneapolis *Star Tribune's* Saturday Home Section, Carlson educates the public on the pleasures of a planet-friendly lifestyle, discussing topics ranging from stylish organic entertaining to nontoxic gardening and eco-golf. She has been featured in *Self, Health, Shape, Natural Health, Cooking Light, Bride & Groom, Experience Life,* and *Midwest Home.*

Visit Carlson's website at *www.earthsmartconsumer.com.*